Contents

Introduction

Welcome to your *Level 3 Applied Diploma in Criminology* textbook!

This is a brief introduction to give you a quick overview. You probably want to get started on the criminology, but it's worth spending a few minutes first to get to know the key features of your book and how you will be assessed.

Your book's features

If you leaf through your book, you will see some of its main features, including the following.

Topics The book's Units are divided into self-contained Topics, each covering one of the assessment criteria that you need to study.

Getting started Each Topic begins with a short activity to get you thinking about that Topic and to link it back to what you have already learned. Some are to be done with a partner or in a small group and others are for you to do on your own.

Activities Within the Topics you will find a wide variety of Activities to develop your knowledge, understanding and skills. Most of these are online (you'll see links to our website). Some are media-based, others are research or discussion-based, and most are to be done in pairs or groups.

Boxes These contain additional information linked to the main text.

Case studies and Scenarios These involve real-life and fictitious cases and crime situations for you to consider.

Questions You will find questions to get you reflecting on what you have read.

Controlled Assessment Preparation At the end of every Unit 1 Topic, a special section outlines what you need to do to prepare for the controlled assessment. You will find a description of what the controlled assessment involves below.

Now Test Yourself At the end of every Unit 2 Topic, you will find one or more practice questions like those you will see in the Unit 2 exam. These will either have Advice on how to tackle the question, or a student's answer that scored in the top mark band, plus the marker's comments.

Studying Level 3 Criminology

This book – *Criminology Book One* – is designed to help you achieve the WJEC Level 3 Applied Certificate or Diploma in Criminology.

- For the Certificate, you must pass Units 1 and 2. These are covered in this book.
- For the Diploma, you must also pass Units 3 and 4. These are covered in *Criminology Book Two*.

These are the Units you will study in your first year:
- **Unit 1 Changing awareness of crime**
- **Unit 2 Criminological theories**

CRIMINOLOGY ONE

for the WJEC Level 3 Certificate & Diploma

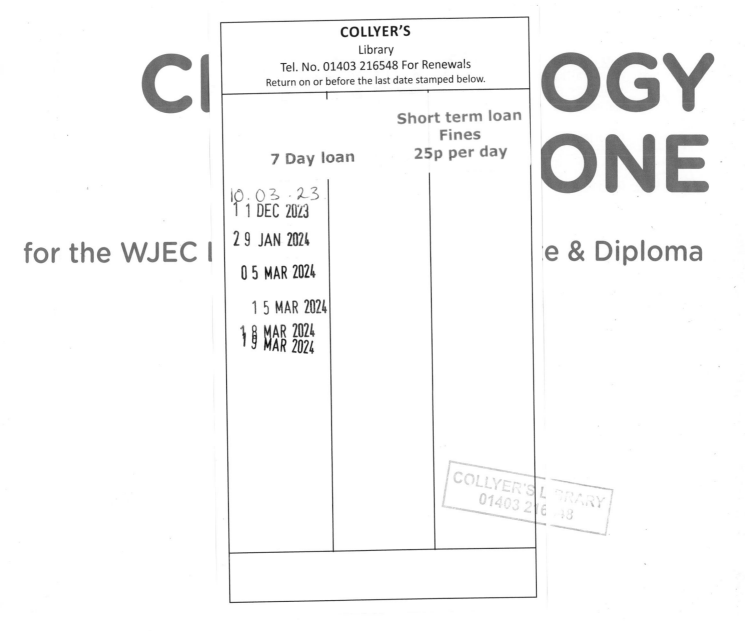

Rob Webb
Annie Townend

NAPIER PRESS **Criminology**

Published by Napier Press Limited
admin@napierpress.com
www.criminology.uk.net

Second edition © Napier Press Limited 2021
First edition published in 2019 by Napier Press Limited

ISBN-13: 9871838271503
ISBN-10: 1838271503

Rob Webb and Annie Townend assert their moral right to be identified as the authors of this work.

British Library Cataloguing in Publication Data
A catalogue record for this book is available from the British Library.

Design by Global Blended Learning
Cover design by Promo Design

Printed sustainably in the UK by Pureprint. This publication has been printed on Amadeus Silk, an FSC® certified paper from responsible sources. This ensures that there is an audited chain of custody from the tree in the well managed forest through to the finished document in the printing factory.

Endorsement statement by WJEC
This material has been endorsed by WJEC and offers high quality support for the delivery of WJEC qualifications. While this material has been through a WJEC quality assurance process, all responsibility for the content remains with the publisher. WJEC bears no responsibility for the example answers to questions taken from its past question papers which are contained in this publication or any judgments on marking bands. WJEC examination questions are used under licence from WJEC CBAC Ltd.

For online support for Criminology teachers and students using this book, including schemes of work, activities and student workbooks.

Go to www.criminology.uk.net

These are the Units you will study in your second year:
- **Unit 3 Crime scene to courtroom**
- **Unit 4 Crime and punishment**

Learning Outcomes

Each unit is divided into Learning Outcomes. These state what you should know, understand and be able to do as a result of completing the Unit. There are three Learning Outcomes for Unit 1 and four for Unit 2.

Assessment Criteria

Each Learning Outcome is divided into Assessment Criteria. There are eleven of these for Unit 1 and ten for Unit 2. They state what you must be able to do in order to show that you have achieved the Learning Outcomes.

In this book, each Assessment Criterion is covered in a separate Topic. For example, Assessment Criterion AC1.1 is covered by Topic 1.1 and so on.

If you look at the Contents page of this book, you will see the Learning Outcomes for Units 1 and 2 and underneath each one, the relevant Assessment Criteria (these are listed as Topics).

How you will be assessed

In the first year of the Diploma course, you will take a controlled assessment and an external exam. The details of these are as follows.

Unit 1: the controlled assessment

- Unit 1 is assessed using a controlled assessment. Just like in a traditional exam, you work alone.
- But unlike in a traditional exam, you may take your class notes into the controlled assessment environment to assist you. Class notes are those supplied by your teacher (in note or PowerPoint form) as well as your personal notes and work from your studies and lessons. You are not permitted to take previously designed materials for Learning Outcome 3 into the controlled assessment.
- The controlled assessment is in two parts. Part one covers Learning Outcome 1 and is three hours long. Part two covers Learning Outcomes 2 and 3 and is five hours long.
- Once you have taken in all your materials on the first day, you must leave them there until the controlled assessment is finished.
- You can use the internet in part two of the assessment, but you won't be allowed to access your own electronic files and documents.
- Your teacher will decide when your class will take the controlled assessment.
- The controlled assessment will be marked by your teacher. A sample of the marked work will then be sent to WJEC, the exam board, to check that it has been marked at the correct standard.
- The assessment includes a brief – a scenario describing a situation involving various crimes. You have to complete certain tasks linked to the brief.

Unit 2: the external exam

- Unit 2 is examined by a traditional exam of 1 hour 30 minutes, set and marked by examiners outside your school or college.
- There are three questions each worth 25 marks – a total of 75 marks.
- Each question is sub-divided into part questions. Some of these will be shorter (1 to 4 marks) and others will be longer (6 or 9 marks).

- Each question begins with stimulus material such as a crime scenario. Some of the part questions will relate to this.
- You sit the exam in the summer term. It will assess all four Learning Outcomes.

Unit 2 and synoptic assessment

Synoptic assessment involves making links between what you learn in different Units, and you will find that some of the questions in the Unit 2 exam will ask about things you have covered in Unit 1.

Grades and re-sits

Both units are graded from A to E.

For Unit 1, you are allowed one re-sit opportunity. If you re-sit, you must submit a new assessment.

For Unit 2, you are allowed two re-sit opportunities. The highest grade will count towards your final overall grade.

Further guidance on assessment

You will find further guidance on the controlled assessment at the end of Unit 1 and on the exam at the end of Unit 2.

Units 3 and 4

In the second year of your course, you will study Units 3 and 4. You will find more detail of these two Units in *Criminology Book Two*.

The Certificate and Diploma units and how they are assessed are summarised below.

Year	Unit	Assessment	Qualification
1	Unit 1 Changing awareness of crime	Controlled assessment 2 parts: 3 hours + 5 hours	25% of the Diploma 50% of the Certificate
1	Unit 2 Criminological theories	Exam 1 hour 30 minutes	25% of the Diploma 50% of the Certificate
2	Unit 3 Crime scene to courtroom	Controlled assessment 2 parts: 3 hours + 5 hours	25% of the Diploma
2	Unit 4 Crime and punishment	Exam 1 hour 30 minutes	25% of the Diploma

CHANGING AWARENESS OF CRIME

Overview

We begin this Unit by looking at a range of different types of crime and then we go on to examine the reasons why some types of crime are under-reported. For example, victims of crimes such as domestic abuse are often reluctant to come forward, while witnesses may decide turn a blind eye to crimes that they view as harmless, such as smoking cannabis or illegally downloading music.

We then go on to examine the effects of crime not being reported. For example, unreported crimes may cease to be a priority for the police, even if the offences involved are serious.

Much of what we know about crime comes from the media, which produce an endless stream of news about real-life crime as well as fictional portrayals in crime dramas. But the media have been accused of distorting and sensationalising crime. In this Unit we look at how accurate the media's portrayal actually is and how it can even make the problem worse, for example by triggering 'moral panics' about crime.

Instead of the media, an alternative source of information are the statistics gathered by the police, government researchers and criminologists. We examine the strengths and limitations of these methods of measuring the amount and types of crime in society.

We then look at what campaigners have done to raise awareness of crimes and how some have succeeded in changing the law. Finally, this Unit gives you the opportunity to practise designing campaign materials and on the day of the controlled assessment, you will design a campaign related to one of the crimes in the brief.

Analyse different types of crime

Getting Started

Working on your own

1. Make a list of five crimes that you have heard about recently - these could be in your local area, nationally reported or even international.

2. For each of the crimes you have listed, which people are the victims of this type of crime and who are the perpetrators (those who commit it)?

3. Why do you think certain kinds of crime receive a lot of media attention?

Share your answers with the person next to you. Do you have similar or different answers?

There are many different crimes. To make sense of crimes, we can group them into different types. This Topic will look at a range of different types of crime.

White collar crime

White collar crimes are crimes that are committed by people who are in a position of power or authority.

Criminal offences

White collar crime covers a wide range of offences by businesses and professionals, including defrauding customers, tax evasion, breaking health and safety laws, polluting the environment, and illegally discriminating against their employees.

Victims and offenders

The criminologist Edwin Sutherland defined white collar crime as: 'a crime committed by a person of respectability and high social status in the course of their occupation'.

This can include people such as company directors and managers, as well as professionals such as accountants, lawyers, doctors and dentists.

- **Corporate crime** When crime is committed by or on behalf of a company (for example, by cheating its customers or evading tax to increase its profits), this is known as corporate crime.

- **Professional crime** When crime is committed by professionals (for example, accountants stealing their clients' funds), this is known as professional crime.

Victims White collar crime is sometimes said to be 'victimless' but in fact there are many victims:

- **Consumers** For example, companies may make false claims when advertising their products, or sell unfit or dangerous goods.

- **Tax payers and the government** Companies who evade tax are defrauding other taxpayers and depriving the government of funds to pay for public services.

- **Employees** For example, employers may subject their workers to bullying, sexual harassment or racial discrimination. Criminologist Steve Tombs calculates that as many as 1,100 work-related deaths a year result from employers breaking the law.
- **The public at large** We all suffer when companies pollute the environment, for example through illegally dumping toxic waste or by selling cars that breach emissions standards.

Box 1   Links to organised crime

When we think of organised crime by groups such as the Mafia, we probably think of violence – for example, running 'protection rackets' or fighting 'turf wars' with other criminal gangs.

However, organised crime often also involves white collar crimes such as money laundering, where the proceeds of crimes such as drug dealing are 'laundered' or cleaned up by being invested in legitimate businesses. This shows how different types of crime are often linked.

Level of public awareness

White collar crime is often said to be 'invisible' – public awareness of it is relatively low compared with street crimes such as assault or burglary. There are several reasons for this:

- **Media coverage** of white collar crime is very limited.
- **Under-reporting** Victims often don't report white collar crime because they don't know they have been victimised, don't regard it as a real crime, or feel it won't make any difference.
- **De-labelling** Offences are often labelled as breaches of regulations rather than crimes.
- **Complexity** Financial crimes are often complex and law enforcers may lack the resources and expertise to investigate them effectively.
- **Power and respectability** The criminals' high status means they are less likely to be suspected and may have the power and wealth to avoid prosecution.

Deviant, criminal or both?

White collar crimes are criminal – they involve breaking the criminal law. But as we have just seen, sometimes they don't appear so because they are invisible or are labelled as breaches of regulations rather than 'real' crimes.

White collar crimes are also deviant and can cause great harm. They often involve a betrayal of trust, such as when lawyers swindle their clients or doctors abuse their patients. For example, the GP Dr Harold Shipman is believed to have murdered at least 218 of his patients. In Sutherland's view, the betrayal of trust makes white collar crime even more deviant than ordinary crime because it undermines faith in vital institutions such as health care.

ACTIVITY / Media

White collar crime   Go to www.criminology.uk.net

Moral crimes

Moral crimes (also called crimes against morality) are acts that go against society's norms or moral code – its accepted values and rules of behaviour.

Criminal offences

Examples of moral crimes include prostitution, selling or possessing illegal drugs, begging, vagrancy and under-age drinking or cigarette smoking. Often, moral crimes involve one person supplying goods (e.g. drugs) or services (e.g. prostitution) to another.

Victims and offenders

Moral crimes are usually considered victimless because there is no specific victim, especially when they involve consenting adults. As a result, there are often no immediate victims to report the crime. For example, a drugs purchaser is unlikely to report himself or the drug dealer to the police.

However, some moral crimes, such as under-age cigarette smoking, do not involve consenting adults and they do have an identifiable victim who needs the protection of the law. It can also be argued that some adults involved in moral crimes are also victims. For example, some women become prostitutes in order to fund their drug addiction, and may be being exploited by a pimp.

Offenders vary according to the particular crime. For some (such as drug dealers), it may be as a source of income or just part of their day-to-day business (such as shopkeepers who sell cigarettes to children). Some may be forced into offending due to personal circumstances, such as beggars and rough sleepers (vagrants).

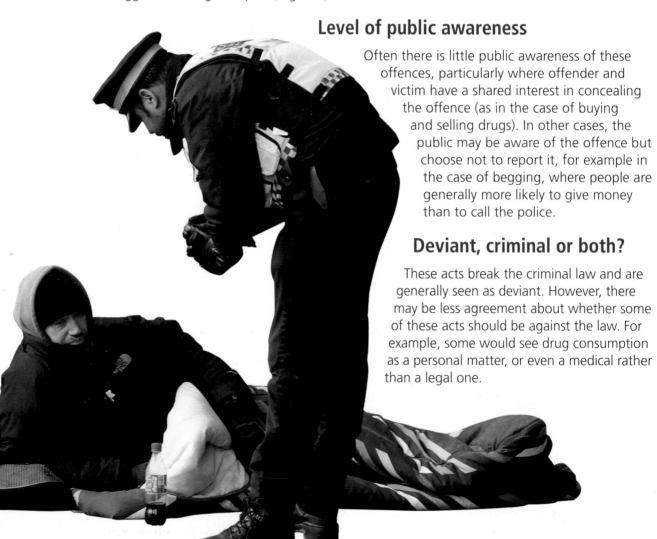

Level of public awareness

Often there is little public awareness of these offences, particularly where offender and victim have a shared interest in concealing the offence (as in the case of buying and selling drugs). In other cases, the public may be aware of the offence but choose not to report it, for example in the case of begging, where people are generally more likely to give money than to call the police.

Deviant, criminal or both?

These acts break the criminal law and are generally seen as deviant. However, there may be less agreement about whether some of these acts should be against the law. For example, some would see drug consumption as a personal matter, or even a medical rather than a legal one.

Rough sleeper. Should vagrancy be a crime?

State crime

Criminologists Green and Ward define state crime as illegal or deviant activities perpetrated by state agencies. They also include crimes by other individuals or groups when carried out with the backing of the state.

Criminal offences

State crimes include human rights abuses such as genocide – the extermination of entire national, ethnic, racial or religious groups. For example, the Nazi state sought to kill all Jews and Roma (Gypsies) in the countries they controlled during the Second World War. In Rwanda in 1994, 800,000 minority Tutsis were murdered by the Hutu-dominated state's forces and by government-backed militias (armed civilian groups).

Other state crimes include:

- **torture** to extract confessions or information from prisoners
- **police brutality**, e.g. assaulting peaceful protestors
- **imprisonment without trial** of political opponents
- **war crimes**, e.g. indiscriminate bombing of the civilian population
- **political crimes** such as election-rigging and corruption by politicians.

Victims and offenders

Victims may be citizens of the state in question, or of another state that has been subject to aggression or occupation by a foreign state. Victims are often members of a religious or ethnic minority (such as the Rwandan Tutsis) or political opponents of the government.

Offenders are state officials such as politicians, civil servants, police officers and the security forces. Offenders also include militias and government supporters acting with the encouragement of the state. In Rwanda, most of the killing was done by militias rather than the state's own security forces.

Offenders can be very senior, such as the leaders of the Nazi party who were prosecuted for war crimes and crimes against humanity at the Nuremberg Trials after the Second World War. But they can also be low-ranking officials such as concentration camp guards or ordinary soldiers.

Level of public awareness

The scale of state crimes is often huge, as in Rwanda, and so the public are likely to be aware of such cases, especially if the media give the crimes full coverage. However, states are powerful and often able to conceal their crimes, for example through censoring the media or by passing laws that legitimise (justify) their actions. Likewise, war crimes of the defeated are more likely to come to light and be punished than those committed by the victors.

Deviant, criminal or both?

Actions such as war crimes, genocide, torture and police brutality are clearly deviant – they go against widely accepted standards of behaviour. On most definitions, they are also crimes. However, states make their own laws and can choose to define their actions as not criminal. For example, the Nazis created laws permitting the state to forcibly sterilise disabled people.

On the other hand, international law defines such human rights abuses as crimes. The International Criminal Court can try those accused of genocide, war crimes and crimes against humanity.

Case study · Genocide

The following are examples of genocide in recent times.

- **The Nazi regime and the Holocaust, Europe 1933-45:** The persecution and killing of the Jews, Roma (Gypsies), gays, the disabled and others by the Nazis.
- **Rwanda, 1994:** 800,000 Tutsis and moderate Hutus were killed, and an unknown number forced to flee the country.
- **Myanmar (Burma) since 2016:** The Rohingya ethnic minority have suffered looting and burning of villages, massacres, sexual violence and expulsion from the country by the military.

ACTIVITY · State crimes

In small groups, research one of these examples and prepare a short presentation to show the rest of the class.

Ethnic cleansing. Rohingya refugees forced out of their homeland in Myanmar.

Technological crimes

These are offences involving the use of information and communication technology (ICT) such as the internet, social media etc. They are also known as cyber-crimes or e-crimes.

Criminal offences

Criminal offences involving ICT include the following:

- **Financial crimes**, e.g. phishing frauds
- **Cyber-trespass**, e.g. hacking social media accounts or releasing viruses
- **Identity theft** (stealing someone's personal data)
- **Hate crimes** such as racist abuse, online threats to rape or assault individuals etc.
- **Illegal downloading** of copyrighted material such as music and videos
- **Publishing or viewing child pornography**.

Data breaches can threaten millions of social media users.

Victims and offenders

More or less anyone with access to the technology is in a position to commit some of these crimes, such as cyber-bullies and stalkers who commit hate crimes on social media. But crimes such as hacking may require specialist technical know-how. Because of the globalised nature of the internet, the offender may be in a different part of the world from the victim.

Victims Anyone who uses the internet is potentially a victim, but more vulnerable groups such as the old and the less educated may be easier prey for financial fraudsters. Even individuals who don't use the internet or social media can still be victims of malicious postings, such as racist abuse. A survey conducted by youth volunteering charity *vInspired* of 2,000 14-18 year olds found that a quarter had been victims of online abuse. Owners of publishing rights (e.g. to music, films or books) may also be victims of internet piracy and breach of copyright.

ACTIVITY / **Research**

Technological crimes

Go to www.criminology.uk.net

Level of public awareness

Awareness of technological crimes varies. Victims are likely to be aware of being trolled, but victims of cyber-fraud or identity theft may not discover for some time that they have been victimised. Public awareness of the risk posed by cyber-crimes varies – some people are more 'internet-savvy' than others – but police, businesses and government have run campaigns to raise awareness and encourage people to take precautions.

Deviant, criminal or both?

Many of these actions are clearly both criminal and deviant, such as viewing child pornography or defrauding people – they are against the law as well as against generally accepted norms of behaviour.

However, some actions, such as illegal downloading of music, may be criminal but they are widely practised and not considered deviant, at least by large sections of society.

Other actions, such as viewing adult pornography, might be regarded as deviant, without being illegal. Likewise, not all trolling is illegal: some actions may be just deviant (e.g. being rude about a person's appearance), but others are both deviant and illegal (e.g. racist abuse or threats).

Case study **Women and cybercrime**

Although anyone can be a victim of cybercrime, a report by the European Institute for Gender Equality (EIGE) found that women and girls are more likely to be victims of cyber violence. The report also notes that although this violence is happening online, it is often linked to offline activities. 77% of women who have experienced cyber harassment have also experienced at least one form of sexual or physical violence from a partner, while 70% of women who have experienced cyber stalking, have also experienced at least one form of physical or sexual violence from a partner.

Adapted from *'Cyber violence is a growing threat, especially for women and girls'*, European Institute for Gender Equality, 19 June 2017

1. Why are women more likely to be victims of cyber violence?

2. Why should this type of crime be reported and investigated?

Individual crimes: hate crime

Hate crimes are crimes where the perpetrator is perceived to be motivated by hatred of the victim because of the victim's disability, race, religion, sexual orientation or transgender identity. These characteristics are known as 'protected characteristics'. The person perceiving the offender to be motivated by hatred doesn't need to be the victim; it can be a witness, the police or anyone else.

Criminal offences

A hate crime can include verbal abuse, intimidation, threats, harassment, assault and bullying, as well as damage to property. Any crime can be aggravated (made worse) if it also involves hate and prosecutors can apply for an increased sentence. For example, if an assault is religiously aggravated, the maximum sentence rises from six months to two years.

Victims and offenders

Offenders tend to be people who hold prejudiced attitudes (such as racism, Islamophobia, transphobia or homophobia) about the group to which the victim belongs.

Anyone who has any of the protected characteristics could potentially be a victim of hate crime. For example, the Crime Survey for England and Wales estimates that on average there are over 100,000 race hate incidents a year against members of minority ethnic groups.

Level of public awareness

There has been greater public awareness of hate crime in recent years. This has been due to an increased focus on reporting, investigating and prosecuting hate crimes. For example, the number of convictions for disability hate crime rose from 141 in 2008 to 800 in 2017.

There has also been increased media interest, particularly in relation to hate crimes committed on social media, and in 2017 the Crown Prosecution Service (the body responsible for bringing prosecutions against offenders) tightened up the guidelines for charging offenders who use social media to commit hate crimes. The work of voluntary organisations such as TellMAMA has also been important in encouraging victims to report offences.

CPS hate crime poster.

ACTIVITY Research

Hate crime   Go to www.criminology.uk.net

Deviant, criminal or both?

Hate crimes are clearly against the criminal law and it is also widely regarded as deviant behaviour to victimise a person because of their race, religion, disability, sexual orientation or gender identity.

Individual crimes: 'honour' crime

So-called 'honour' crimes (also called 'honour-based violence') involve violence committed to defend the supposed honour of a family or community. The violence is directed against the individual who is deemed to have brought shame on the family.

Criminal offences

'Honour' crimes include threatening behaviour, assault, wounding, burning, acid attacks and disfiguration, abduction, rape and murder. In the UK there are 12 'honour' killings a year on average.

'Honour' crimes may also involve family or community members in a conspiracy to commit or conceal the crime, or to protect the perpetrator. (A conspiracy is where individuals collaborate to plan, commit or cover up a crime.)

Forced marriage A related crime is forced marriage, where a person does not freely give consent but marries under duress (pressure), usually from family members. It may also involve forcing a person to leave the UK with the intention of making them marry a partner abroad chosen by the family.

Many people also see female genital mutilation (FGM) as an 'honour' crime aimed at controlling the sexuality of the victim.

Victims and offenders

'Honour' crimes are usually perpetrated by the victims' families, extended families and members of their community. Most commonly the offenders are male relatives – fathers, brothers, uncles or cousins – but female relatives may also be involved.

Often, families commit 'honour' crimes as a result of pressure from their community and the fear of losing their good name if they fail to punish the individual concerned.

Almost all victims are female. Most are young. In the UK, most victims are from minority ethnic groups, particularly Asian communities.

Girls and young women in some communities are expected to remain virgins until they marry, to not develop relationships outside their community, and to accept their family's decision about who they will marry. Those who are suspected of not doing so are more likely to be victims of 'honour' crimes. Married women who seek divorce or custody of their children are also more likely to be targeted.

ACTIVITY Research

'Honour' crimes   Go to www.criminology.uk.net

Level of public awareness

Public awareness has been relatively low because the communities involved may see 'honour' crimes as justified. However, the number of crimes reported to the police is now increasing, especially since forced marriage became a crime in 2014, which has raised awareness of 'honour' crimes. Over 5,000 crimes are now reported each year.

However, although more victims are coming forward, the police only refer about 5% of cases to the Crown Prosecution Service (CPS) for prosecution. Women's charities also say that cuts to legal aid and to support services for women from minority communities have left many victims unable to get justice or protection.

Deviant, criminal or both?

Honour-based violence is criminal behaviour that violates the victim's right to choose how to live her life. Wider society also regards this as deviant behaviour, since it is not accepted that families should be able to control a woman's behaviour by the use of violence.

However, within some communities, gender norms mean that women are expected to behave in certain ways and to face punishment if they fail to conform. Yet as the CPS points out, 'there is no honour or justification for abusing the human rights of others'.

Individual crimes: domestic abuse

Domestic abuse (also called domestic violence) involves the use of violence, abuse or threatening behaviour against a partner, ex-partner or family member.

Criminal offences

The law applies to those aged 16 and over, regardless of gender or sexuality. It includes the following types of abuse:

- **Physical and sexual assaults and rape**.
- **Financial abuse**, e.g. controlling the victim's money or running up debts in their name.
- **Emotional or psychological abuse**, e.g. intimidation and threats, constant undermining and criticism, being made to feel guilty.

As well as laws against physical and sexual violence, since 2015 there has also been an offence of coercive or controlling behaviour:

- **Controlling behaviour** is designed to make the victim subordinate or dependent, e.g. by isolating them, controlling their daily life, exploiting them financially or preventing them from escaping the relationship.
- **Coercive behaviour** involves emotional abuse to harm, punish or frighten the victim.

Clare's Law (the Domestic Violence Disclosure Scheme) gives women the right to ask police to check whether their partner has a violent past. It is named after Clare Wood, who was murdered in 2009 by her ex-boyfriend, who had an undisclosed history of violence. For more about Clare's Law, see Unit 2, Topic 4.3.

Victims and offenders

The great majority of offenders are male. Offenders are usually the partner or ex-partner of the victim, although other family members can also be perpetrators.

Most victims are female. Research also shows that female victims are more likely to suffer multiple types of abuse and more severe violence and control.

However, some women are more at risk than others. According to the Crime Survey for England and Wales (CSEW), the following groups of women were at greater risk: those aged

16-24; separated and divorced women; lone parents; those with a disability; and women in the lowest income bracket.

Males are less likely to be victims and male victims are even less likely than female victims to report abuse. This may be due to the feeling that it is unmasculine and to the fact that the abuse is generally less severe.

ACTIVITY / Media

Domestic abuse   Go to www.criminology.uk.net

Level of public awareness

Several factors lead to low public awareness of domestic abuse:

- It takes place mainly in the home, hidden from the public and police.
- Victims are often too afraid to report the crime, which makes the problem look smaller than it really is.
- The police have often seen it as 'only a domestic' and not intervened in what they view as a private matter between man and wife.

However, feminist campaigners have had some success bringing domestic abuse to the attention of the media, politicians and the public, and this has pushed the criminal justice system into taking it more seriously. However, there remains a long way to go. For example, the CSEW found that 1.6 million women suffered domestic abuse in 2020. Yet only a small minority of these offences are reported to police and only 1 in 12 of these results in a successful prosecution.

Deviant, criminal or both?

Domestic abuse is a crime and is widely accepted as being deviant behaviour. However, the CSEW found that a small minority of both men and women thought it was acceptable to hit or slap a partner in certain circumstances, such as having an affair or cheating on them, flirting with other people, or constantly nagging.

CONTROLLED ASSESSMENT PREPARATION

What you have to do

Using your notes from Topic 1.1 *Analyse different types of crime*, analyse the following types of crime, using a range of relevant examples:

- white collar: organised; corporate; professional
- moral
- state: human rights

- technological: e-crime
- individual: hate crime; honour crime; domestic abuse

Use the following points to analyse each type of crime:

- criminal offences
- types of victim
- types of offender

- level of public awareness
- criminal, deviant or both.

The assignment brief scenario

You must analyse two crimes in the assignment brief, which you will be given on the day of the controlled assessment.

How it will be marked

3-4 marks: Analysis of two types of crime evident in the assignment brief.

1-2 marks: Description of two types of crime evident in the assignment brief.

Explain the reasons that certain crimes are unreported

Getting started

Working in small groups

1. List five crimes which you or someone you know could be a victim of.

2. For each of these crimes, give a reason why the victim might not report the crime.

3. Each group should give feedback to the rest of the class. Make a list of all the reasons from the class.

Reasons for unreported crime

Crimes can only be investigated and solved if they are reported to the police. There are many reasons why crimes are not reported. For example, a person may be unaware that they are the victim of a crime. On the other hand, they may be well aware they are a victim but may have personal, social or cultural reasons for not reporting the crime.

Personal reasons

There are several personal reasons why some people may not report a crime.

Fear

The victim of a crime may be concerned that there will be reprisals if they report it to the police. If the victim knows the offender, they may be afraid that reporting the crime might lead to further actions against them. Victims may also fear the possible consequences for their families and those close to them.

> **Scenario Fear**
>
> John is having a drink in a local bar with his girlfriend. A group of local men enter the bar. A man (Steve) from the group approaches the bar at the same time as John to buy drinks. John gets served by the bartender. Steve is angry that John was served first and he threatens both John and the bartender. After a scuffle, where John sustains a slight injury, the group of men manage to calm Steve and get him away from the bar.
>
> 1. Why might John be afraid to report the assault?
> 2. Why might the bartender not report the assault?

Shame

Being the victim of a crime may cause embarrassment or shame. The victim may not want to admit that such a crime has happened because of how it makes them feel or how it makes them appear to others. As a result, they may fail to report the crime to the police.

Scenario **Shame**

Michelle was on a night out with girlfriends. In the nightclub, the women started chatting to a group of men. One of the men, Mark, seemed interested in Michelle. She chatted with him and let him buy her a drink. After that, things were a little hazy for Michelle. The next thing she remembers is waking up in her flat. She was naked and realised that someone else was in the flat. Michelle could not remember getting home. Mark appeared from the bathroom, got dressed and left. He gave Michelle his number and suggested they meet up again sometime.

1. Why do you think Michelle did not report what happened? Give as many reasons as possible.
2. Suggest reasons why it would be a good idea for Michelle to report the events of the night to the police.

Disinterest

A crime may go unreported because those who witness it are disinterested. For example, if someone witnesses adolescents drinking alcohol in the local park, they may be unconcerned about the offence being committed and so do not bother to report it.

Scenario **Disinterest**

Sam is 21 and lives in an inner-city area with a lot of flats. Most people in the area do not have their own garden but there is a community park for residents. There used to be a community centre and a youth club, but these have closed. Young people in the area now gather in the park, especially during school holidays. Many of the young people drink alcohol and some smoke both cigarettes and cannabis. Sam often sees the youths in the park on his way home from work.

1. Suggest reasons why Sam may not report the underage smoking and drinking in the park.
2. Would everyone in the neighbourhood feel the same as Sam? Suggest other residents who might be more likely to report these actions.

Not affected by the crime

Similarly to being disinterested, a person may not be personally affected by a particular crime and so may not feel the need to report it to the police. For example, if a person sees someone else's car or home being broken into, they may not care because it doesn't affect them personally and so they don't report it.

Question

In the scenario on disinterest above, why might Sam not be affected by the young people?

Social and cultural reasons

As well as personal reasons for not reporting crime, social and cultural factors may play a part.

Lack of knowledge

One reason for not reporting a crime is that people may not know that a particular action is against the law and so they do not consider reporting it.

Similarly, they may lack the knowledge of how to make a report or to whom they should make it. For example, if someone receives abusive or threatening messages online, they may not know what they need to do to report this crime. If no face-to-face personal contact has occurred a victim may not realise that these actions can still be dealt with by the authorities.

ACTIVITY Research

ACTIVITY Research

Reporting online bullying　　　　　　　　　Go to www.criminology.uk.net

Complexity

Some crimes are very complex and it can be difficult to tell whether a crime has been committed. For example, white collar crimes committed in companies may involve complex accounting procedures which mean the crime is never uncovered. Clearly, if a crime is not discovered in the first place, then it cannot be reported.

Case study | Complexity of the crime

For two and a half years, an accountant, a construction services company boss and a payroll administrator defrauded HM Revenue and Customs (HMRC) of VAT, income tax and National Insurance Contributions deductions worth £6.9 million.

The men hid their fraud by using a complex network of companies and bank accounts. Clients of the company were charged VAT on the services provided, employees of the company had tax deducted from their pay, but neither the VAT nor the taxes were paid across to HMRC.

The company supplied short-term contractors to the construction industry, often providing hundreds of workers at a time. But rather than pay the tax and National Insurance to HMRC, the three men stole the money to fund lavish lifestyles.

Adapted from HMRC Press Release, 24 October 2016

1. Why would it be difficult to know that the men in this case had committed a crime?

2. Why would this type of crime be unlikely to be reported?

Lack of media interest

Much of our knowledge of crime is gained through the media's coverage of it. This increases people's awareness and may make witnesses and victims of the sorts of crimes covered by the media more likely to report them to the police.

Conversely, crimes that are not in the media spotlight may not get reported to the police. If the media don't sensitise their audiences to a given type of crime, the public will be less vigilant or anxious about it and less likely to notice it, and less likely to report it if they do notice it.

However, if the media start to take an interest in a certain type of crime, this will increase the crime's profile and may encourage victims of similar offences to report them.

ACTIVITY Research

The impact of media interest　　　　　　　Go to www.criminology.uk.net

Lack of current public concern

Similarly to a lack of media interest, if a crime is not causing public concern then it is less likely people will report it. For example, public attitudes to cannabis have changed over the years and many people now see it as relatively harmless, despite the fact that possession of the drug remains a crime. (A YouGov survey in 2019 found a slight majority in favour of legalising its possession.) As a result, they are unlikely to report it to the police.

Case study | Lack of public concern

The *Independent* reported in 2016 that 47% of people in the UK supported the licensed sale of cannabis. Part of the reason for support from the public and from some politicians is the estimated £1 billion in tax that would be generated from sales. This would also mean this money is not in the hands of criminals.

1. What advantages does this suggest there would be from legalising cannabis?
2. What reasons might there be for not supporting legalisation?
3. What do you think would be the impact on crime if cannabis were legalised?
4. What other activities can you suggest that are against the law but that the public may not be concerned about?

Weed World market stall, Glastonbury Festival. Are the public no longer concerned about cannabis?

Culture-bound crime

The United Kingdom is a multicultural society with a range of different beliefs and cultural practices. The cultural practices of some groups may break the law. Examples of cultural practices that are against the law in the UK are female genital mutilation and forced marriage.

While such practices are criminal, the fact that they are linked to the culture and customs of some communities may mean they are not reported to the police. For members of the community in question, this may be because they see no wrong in the activity. Alternatively, they may fear reprisals from their own community if they report the crime. Those outside the community may feel that they should not interfere in other people's cultures.

Scenario | Culture-bound crime

Aaminah is 14 and her family are from Pakistan. She was born in the UK and has never been to Pakistan. She is the eldest of three sisters. Aaminah wants to stay on at school and get a career.

Aaminah's parents are very strict. Recently her parents have been planning a trip to Pakistan; they say that this is so Aaminah can meet some of her family. Despite this claim, Aaminah is concerned about the trip. She has heard about cases where families have taken their daughters to Pakistan to be married and she is worried that the trip is for her to get married.

1. Why would the family's plans for Aaminah be a crime?
2. Why might Aaminah be unwilling to report the crime? Give as many reasons as you can.

CONTROLLED ASSESSMENT PREPARATION

What you have to do

Using your notes from Topic 1.2 *Explain the reasons that certain crimes are unreported*, give clear and detailed explanation of the reasons using relevant examples.

Reasons

- personal, e.g. fear, shame, disinterest, not affected
- social and cultural, e.g. lack of knowledge; complexity; lack of media interest; lack of current public concern, culture bound crime (e.g. 'honour' killing, witchcraft).

You should consider crimes such as:

- common assault
- domestic abuse
- vandalism

- perceived victimless crimes (e.g. white collar crime, vagrancy, prostitution, assisted suicide).
- rape

The assignment brief scenario

Where a reason you are explaining also appears in the brief, you should make reference to the brief.

How it will be marked

3-4 marks: Clear and detailed explanation of the reasons for the two unreported crimes.

1-2 marks: Reasons for the two unreported crimes are limited in explanation.

Explain the consequences of unreported crime

Getting started

Working with a partner

1. Using your work from Topics 1.1 and 1.2, note down three types of crime that may not be reported and the reasons why they might not be reported.

2. Think of as many consequences (effects) as you can of these types of crime not being reported.

3. Share your answers with the class.

As we saw in the previous Topic, there are many reasons why crimes often go unreported. There are also a number of consequences of crimes going unreported. In this Topic we shall examine them.

The ripple effect

This is based on the idea of a pebble being dropped into a pond, creating ripples that spread out across the pond's surface. In the case of crime, this means that an unreported crime (the 'pebble') may affect not just the immediate or primary victim, but will spread across a whole community or society (the 'ripple') to affect secondary victims. The ripple effect can occur for many types of crime.

Hate crimes An example of the ripple effect can be seen with hate crimes. Ethnic minorities may be victims of hate crimes. Although a crime may be committed against an individual, the message may spread a 'wave of harm' throughout a whole community. This can be particularly true of online abuse in a public forum.

Cultural consequences

People from different cultures sometimes view the same action differently. This may mean that some practices that are seen as unacceptable and are against the law in the UK are acceptable to some people from other cultures.

Female genital mutilation (FGM) may be an example of this. FGM is a crime in the UK but is a common practice in several parts of the world and exists among some minority cultures in the UK. Offenders in these communities may therefore believe they can offend without risk of punishment, leading to continued high rates of offending. As a result, it may go unreported by members of the communities that practise it and be allowed to occur out of sight of the law. According to Haroon Siddique:

> "More than 20,000 girls a year are thought to be at risk of FGM in the UK. Medical groups, trade unions and human rights organisations estimate that there are 66,000 victims of the practice in England and Wales."

However, some members of these communities have spoken out against FGM as a violation of girls' and women's human rights, and professionals such as doctors and teachers have been vigilant to identify victims and girls at risk.

Honour crimes and forced marriages that we considered in Topic 1.1 raise similar issues.

Decriminalisation and legal change

Some actions are widespread in society despite being against the law. For example, large numbers of people use or have used cannabis. However, because many members of the public see it as a relatively harmless, victimless crime, it goes unreported.

When a particular crime becomes widespread and the public stop reporting it because they no longer see it as a 'real' crime, campaigners may demand a change in the law. In the case of cannabis, a number of countries and U.S. states have responded to public pressure by decriminalising its possession. Decriminalisation means it is treated as a misdemeanour: a minor offence, where the penalty may be a warning or small fine.

Legalisation Some countries and U.S. states have gone further and legalised cannabis for recreational or medicinal use. Some countries have also decriminalised possession of 'hard' drugs such as heroin. They argue that this reduces the amount of violent crime associated with the drugs trade, saves money on imprisoning offenders and reduces the spread of HIV infections caused by needle-sharing.

ACTIVITY	Research

Decriminalisation of homosexuality   Go to www.criminology.uk.net

Police prioritisation

Some kinds of crime often go unreported, such as domestic abuse. This may mean that the police are unaware of the scale of the offending and so do not prioritise it. As a result, once the public become aware that the police are not prioritising certain crimes, they are less likely to report these crimes since they believe the police will not deal with them.

The police give priority to some crimes over others. They may do this for several reasons:

- **They have limited resources** and cannot investigate every single crime. Recent government spending cuts have meant police forces have had to make difficult decisions about what crimes to concentrate on.
- **The local population** may have concerns about certain types of crime or anti-social behaviour that they want the police to deal with.
- **The media** may focus on a particular type of crime and call for action by the police.
- **The Home Office** (the central government department responsible for policing) has particular priorities that it wants police forces throughout the country to tackle, such as human trafficking.

Inevitably, this means that some crimes receive lower priority, as in the case of cannabis possession, where police may turn a blind eye. Enforcing the law against such large numbers of offenders would be both unpopular and extremely costly in terms of police resources, which they may prefer to spend tackling more serious crimes.

Case study	Child sexual abuse

In 2012 the police set up Operation Yewtree, following an ITV documentary about sexual abuse committed by the radio and TV broadcaster Jimmy Savile. Operation Yewtree was initially to investigate Savile but was later widened to include other celebrities such as Gary Glitter and Max Clifford. Yewtree was set up in response to members of the public reporting historical cases of sexual abuse by various celebrities following the documentary. As these cases emerged, there was heightened media coverage of Yewtree, especially since the suspects were celebrities.

1. Why would a TV documentary lead to members of the public coming forward to report crime?
2. Why would cases involving celebrities gain greater media coverage?
3. How might police priorities be changed when the media reported cases of historical child sexual abuse?

Unrecorded crime

For a crime to be recorded by the police and then investigated and prosecuted, they must first know that a crime has actually occurred. Although the police do detect some crimes, most crime (up to 90%) is brought to their attention by the public reporting it to them. If people choose not to report crimes, then obviously they cannot be recorded or investigated.

However, even when an alleged crime is reported to the police, they have some discretion and may decide not to record it. This can be for several reasons:

- They may not believe the story or may not have enough evidence to secure a conviction.
- The victim may refuse to press charges.
- They may not wish to investigate, e.g. because the crime is too trivial or not a priority for them, or to save resources or increase clear-up rates.

The dark figure

If the police do not record a crime, it will not appear in the police statistics. These unrecorded crimes are known as the dark figure of crime. This is all the other crime – including the crimes no-one has witnessed, crimes that were witnessed but not reported, and crimes that were reported to the police but not recorded by them.

The absence of unrecorded crime from the official crime statistics recorded by the police means that the government and the criminal justice system get a distorted picture of the patterns of crime in the country, leading them to focus only on the types of crime that appear important from the statistics while neglecting others that may in fact be more widespread or serious.

ACTIVITY / Research

Crime in your area   Go to www.criminology.uk.net

Cultural change

Non-reporting of crime can lead to changes in culture. These include the following changes.

New technology

New technology can bring new opportunities for crime. For example, we now have instant access to a wide range of media. This gives rise to new cybercrimes such as illegal music downloading. These are widely seen as not 'real' crimes and so go unreported. This reinforces the idea that they are acceptable and this behaviour becomes a part of society's culture.

Acceptance of disorder

Another cultural change may occur in neighbourhoods with high rates of petty crime, such as vandalism, graffiti, begging, drug dealing, prostitution and drunkenness. Residents may come to accept this situation, perhaps because they feel helpless to do anything about it, and so they cease to report the crimes. This in turn means the police will fail to record and tackle it. Crime thus becomes the norm in the area and other criminals are attracted to it, creating a downward spiral as it becomes increasingly crime-ridden, run-down and neglected.

'Broken windows' theory by Wilson and Kelling argues that if minor crime goes unreported and is not tackled by the police, this will eventually lead to more serious crime. Wilson and Kelling use 'broken windows' to stand for all the various signs of disorder and lack of concern for others in a neighbourhood. They argue that leaving broken windows unrepaired, tolerating aggressive begging etc. sends out a signal that nobody cares and the area falls into decline.

Wilson and Kelling argue that to halt this decline, we need a twofold strategy:

- **An environmental improvement strategy**: broken windows must be repaired immediately, abandoned cars towed away without delay etc.
- **A zero tolerance policing strategy**: the police must proactively tackle even the slightest sign of disorder (even if it's not criminal).

ACTIVITY Discussion

Broken windows   Go to www.criminology.uk.net

Procedural change

Concerns about the under-reporting of crime may lead to the police making changes in how crimes can be reported. In the past, reporting a crime usually meant either visiting the police station or dialling 999. However, in recent times the police and voluntary organisations have introduced new procedures to make reporting easier. These include:

- **TV programmes** such as Crimewatch.
- **Telephone hotlines** such as CrimeStoppers and ChildLine. These usually allow anonymous reporting.
- **Voluntary organisations** such as Victim Support, Stonewall and TellMAMA offer support to individuals wishing to report a crime.
- **Posters and recorded announcements**, e.g. at stations, such as 'See it, say it, sorted' messages encouraging people to report suspicious items or behaviour.
- **Phone apps** that allow rapid contact with the police in an emergency.

CONTROLLED ASSESSMENT PREPARATION

What you have to do

Using your notes from Topic 1.3 *Explain the consequences of unreported crime*, give clear and detailed explanation (including relevant examples) of all the following consequences of unreported crimes:

- ripple effect
- cultural consequences
- decriminalisation
- police prioritisation
- unrecorded crime
- cultural change
- legal change
- procedural change.

You should have an understanding of the positive and negative effects of unreported crime on the individual and on society.

The assignment brief scenario

Where a consequence you are explaining also appears in the assignment brief in the controlled assessment, you should use examples from the brief or from your own studies.

How it will be marked

3-4 marks: Clear and detailed explanation (includes relevant examples) of the consequences of unreported crimes.
1-2 marks: Limited explanation (may only list examples) of the consequences of unreported crime.

Describe media representation of crime

Getting started

In small groups, collect a range of different newspapers. These could be print copies or online versions. Find at least one of each of the following: a local paper; a national 'red top' tabloid paper (such as the Sun); a national 'quality' paper (such as the Guardian).

1. Find examples of reporting of crimes in each of the newspapers.
2. If any of the papers report the same crimes, compare the stories. Are there differences in the way crimes are reported – for example, the headlines, the language used or the photographs?
3. Do local newspapers report crime differently from national newspapers? This might be different crimes or different styles of reporting. Are there more reports of crime in one type of newspaper than another?
4. Prepare a short presentation to summarise your findings on the reporting of crime in newspapers.

The media and crime

Although we may have direct, personal experience of crime ourselves, much of our knowledge about crime comes indirectly, from the media. There are many different media, including newspapers, novels, films, TV and radio, and social media, all portraying crime, both fictional and real. In this Topic, we shall look at how different media represent crime and criminals.

Newspapers

There are many types of newspaper, including the following:

- The 'popular' press, such as the *Daily Mail*, and the 'quality' press such as the *Guardian*
- Daily papers, plus Sunday papers like the *Observer*
- Local and regional papers such as the *Evening Standard* (London) and the *Western Mail* (Cardiff), and free papers such as the *Metro*.
- All major newspapers now have online as well as print versions. Sales of most papers have been falling for many years.

Crime is big news in the press. One study found that one in eight news reports were about crime, and that the tabloids devoted more space to crime. The tabloids focus on sensational stories and treat them as a form of 'infotainment' – a cross between factual information and fictional entertainment.

News values The kinds of crime, criminals and victims that appear in newspaper reports are in many ways the opposite of those that appear in the official crime statistics. The criminologist Surette calls this 'the law of opposites'. As Box 2 shows, crimes are more likely to be deemed newsworthy if they fit key 'news values'.

Type of crime

Newspapers concentrate on serious violent crimes and sexual crimes – whereas the vast majority of crimes recorded in the official statistics are minor property crimes such as shoplifting. One study found that almost two-thirds of newspaper crime stories featured violence. Homicide features in about a third of all crime reports. The homicides most likely to be reported are those with sex, financial gain, jealousy or revenge as the motive. Tabloids carry more stories involving violence and give them more prominence.

Criminals and victims

In press reports, both offenders and victims are typically older and of higher status than those who turn up in the courts. Reports over-represent children, women, middle-class, White and older people as victims. The only point of agreement between news reports and the official statistics is that both see the typical offender as male.

Ignoring the causes Newspaper stories focus on particular incidents rather than on the overall causes of crime. For example, reports of rape often focus on demonising the individual offender rather than on wider issues of male power. Similarly, crimes involving rioting or terrorism are often reported without explaining the political background to the crimes.

Coverage of the police Press reports tend to exaggerate the success of the police in solving crimes, while crimes committed by police officers are often presented as the work of 'one bad apple' rather than as anything more widespread.

Box 2 | News values

News values are the criteria that journalists and editors use to decide whether a story is newsworthy enough to make it into the paper or news bulletin. If a story can be told in terms of these values, it has a better chance of making the news. News values include:

- **Immediacy** – 'breaking news'
- **Dramatisation** – action and excitement
- **Personalisation** – human interest stories about individuals
- **Higher-status persons** and celebrities
- **Simplification** – eliminating 'shades of grey' in the story
- **Novelty or unexpectedness** – a new 'angle' or a 'shock' development
- **Risk** – victim-centred stories about vulnerability and fear
- **Violence** – especially involving visible and spectacular acts.

Television

While newspapers report 'real' crimes, TV broadcasts both crime news and crime fiction.

Crime news

TV coverage is similar to the papers in terms of a strong focus on violent crime (especially in local news bulletins). Likewise, TV news portrays both offenders and victims as older and more middle-class. However, 'reality' TV shows are an exception: they concentrate more on stories involving young suspects.

Crime fiction

About a quarter of all TV output is devoted to crime dramas. The pattern here is similar to the coverage of crime in news broadcasts.

Violence About two-thirds of U.S. crime shows consist of murder, assault or armed robbery. The motive for murder is often shown as greed and calculation – whereas in reality, most homicides result from domestic conflicts or brawls between young men. Likewise, while most sex crimes are in fact committed by people known to the victim, in TV fiction (and TV news stories) they are committed by psychopathic strangers.

Property crime, when it does appear on TV, is portrayed as more serious than most offences really are, for example as tightly planned, high value thefts, often accompanied by violence.

Offenders and victims Crime dramas generally portray offenders as higher-status, White, middle-aged males. Victims are similar, but a higher proportion are females. In recent years, victims have become more central in both TV and film fiction, and audiences are encouraged to identify with them.

The police TV crime generally has a high clear-up rate, compared with the official crime statistics – the police usually get their man. However, there is a trend towards dramas where the police fail. The police are generally portrayed in a positive light, but there is an increasing tendency to portray brutal or corrupt officers.

ACTIVITY / Research

Crime on TV   Go to www.criminology.uk.net

Film

About a fifth of all cinema films are crime movies and up to half have significant crime content. The pattern of representations in fictional crime is similar to that on TV.

Representation of violence has become more explicit and extreme over time. Property crime is under-represented compared with the official statistics.

After the trial of the two boys accused of murdering two-year-old Jamie Bulger in 1993, it was suggested that one of the defendants might have been influenced in their actions by viewing the 'video nasty', Child's Play 3. However, police who investigated the case found no evidence that this had occurred.

Samuel L. Jackson and John Travolta as hit men in *Pulp Fiction*. But how close is fiction to fact?

ACTIVITY / Media

Crime in film   Go to www.criminology.uk.net

Electronic gaming

Many electronic games involve crime. In 'shoot-'em-up' games such as *Grand Theft Auto* and *Manhunt,* players engage in simulated violence and homicide. In view of the popularity of such games, there has been concern that some people may be becoming 'addicted' to gaming.

For example, in 2018 the World Health Organisation classified 'gaming disorder' as a medical condition involving loss of control over gaming so that it takes priority over a gamer's daily activities and significantly affects their personal, family, social, educational or occupational functioning.

One fear is that heavy users of violent games may become desensitised to violence and regard it as normal, or even perform 'copycat' crimes themselves.

However, despite many studies of the possible effects of exposure to media violence, including in electronic games, there is very little evidence of harmful effects. Concerns about video gaming among children in particular may have more to do with society's desire to regard childhood as a time of innocence than with any real effects gaming actually has. It may even be that such games allow players to release aggressive feelings in a harmless way – a process some psychologists call catharsis.

Social media: blogs and social networking

There are also links between crime and social media. As we saw in Topic 1.1, social media can be used as a means of committing hate crimes such as harassment and racist or homophobic abuse.

There are also cases of gang assaults being staged, recorded and posted online, and then sometimes packaged as underground fight videos. 'Drill rap' videos have also been posted online to provoke conflict with other gangs (see below).

ACTIVITY Research

Performance crimes

Go to www.criminology.uk.net

Preventing crime On the other hand, social media can also be used to prevent or report crime. For example, police forces now have Facebook and Twitter accounts that they use to appeal for information or witnesses, and to alert people to the risks of becoming a victim. The National Crime Agency posts accounts of its work on various social media, including clips of arrests of people involved in serious and organised crime. Police may also search suspects' phones for incriminating evidence in text messages and selfies.

Members of the public can also use social media to raise public awareness by warning others of crimes or risks of becoming victims. Apps such as Witness Evident exist to enable the public to report crime to the police, send photo, video and audio evidence, and make statements. Other apps exist to report specific kinds of crime, such as hate crime.

ACTIVITY Media

Using apps to report crime

Go to www.criminology.uk.net

Music

Crime has been a popular subject for musicians for many years. Vengeful lovers, gangsters, drug dealers, bank robbers, prisoners and many more criminal types have featured in song lyrics.

Some kinds of music may contribute to crime. For example, drill rap videos featuring threatening lyrics have been posted on YouTube. Often aimed at one street gang by another, these music videos have been blamed for inter-gang assaults and murders. In 2018, a court order banned members of the drill group *1011* from mentioning injury or death in their music and required them to notify police when releasing a new video.

Crime as fashion Music and music videos may also turn crime into a commodity and fashion statement. For example, gangster rap and hip hop combine images of street hustler criminality with images of luxury goods and designer chic. Advertising uses hip hop music videos to sell products to young people, packaging and marketing crime as edgy, glamorous and cool.

ACTIVITY / Media

Music and crime
Go to www.criminology.uk.net

CONTROLLED ASSESSMENT PREPARATION

What you have to do
Using your notes from Topic 1.4 *Describe media representation of crime*, give a detailed description of the media representation of crime, including relevant examples.

Media
- newspaper
- television
- film
- electronic gaming
- social media (blogs, social networking)
- music.

You should have knowledge of specific examples of how different forms of media are used to portray fictional and factual representations of crime.

The assignment brief scenario
Where relevant, you should make reference to the brief.

How it will be marked
4-6 marks: Detailed description of the media representation of crime, including relevant examples.
1-3 marks: Limited description of the media representation of crime.

Explain the impact of media representations on the public perception of crime

Getting started

Working with a partner

1. Make a list of three crimes you have seen in the media in the last week.

2. How did you hear about these crimes? Be specific — say what type of media, for example.

3. Would you have heard about these crimes if they were not in the media?

Share your answers with the class. Did everyone have the same stories?

The impact of media portrayals of crime

How the media portray crime and criminals has a big impact on how the public perceives crime. Media coverage can affect how much crime people believe there is, whether they think it is increasing, and how much of a threat they feel it to be. In turn, this may lead the public to demand that the police, courts or government take steps to deal with the perceived problem, such as a 'crackdown' on a particular type of crime or the introduction of new laws.

ACTIVITY / Media

The impact of media coverage   Go to www.criminology.uk.net

Moral panic

The media's representations of crime may actually cause *more* crime by creating a moral panic. Stanley Cohen defines a moral panic as an exaggerated, irrational over-reaction by society to a perceived problem. It starts with the media identifying a group as a *folk devil* or threat to society's values, exaggerating the problem's real seriousness with sensationalised reporting.

The media, politicians and other respectable figures then condemn the group's misbehaviour and call for a 'crackdown' by the authorities. However, this can actually make matters worse, by amplifying (enlarging) the scale of the problem that caused the panic in the first place.

The mods and rockers

Cohen's book *Folk Devils and Moral Panics* is a classic study of this process. Cohen examines how the media's response to disturbances between two groups of working-class youths, the mods and the rockers, created a moral panic.

Initially, differences between the two were not clear cut and not many young people identified themselves as belonging to either 'group'. The disturbances started on a wet Easter weekend in 1964 at the resort of Clacton, with a few scuffles and some minor property damage.

However, the media's over-reaction triggered a moral panic. This involved three elements:

- **Exaggeration and distortion** of the numbers involved and the seriousness of the trouble, distorting the picture with sensational headlines.
- **Prediction** that further conflict and violence would occur.
- **Symbolisation** Symbols of the mods and rockers, such as their clothes, hairstyles, bikes and scooters, were negatively labelled.

A group of mods arriving in Clacton, closely watched by police.

ACTIVITY / Media

Moral panic   Go to www.criminology.uk.net

The deviance amplification spiral

Leslie Wilkins argues that the media can produce a deviance amplification spiral – a process where attempts by the authorities to control deviance actually produce *more* deviance, not less, leading to further attempts at control and yet more deviance.

In the case of the mods and rockers, the media did this in two ways:

- Media coverage made it appear that the problem was getting out of hand and this led to calls for a stronger 'control response' or crackdown from the police and courts. This increased the stigmatisation (negative labelling) of the mods and rockers as criminals.
- The media emphasised the supposed differences between the two groups. This encouraged more youths to identify with one group and see the other as their enemy, fuelling further clashes. This created a self-fulfilling prophecy where youths acted out the roles the media had assigned to them, increasing the scale of the disturbances and producing an even tougher response from the authorities, with more arrests and harsher sentences.

Since the mods and rockers, there have been numerous other folk devils and moral panics that share some of the features described by Cohen. Possible examples include drug use, homosexuality and HIV/Aids, Islamist terrorism, football hooliganism, muggings, child sexual abuse, dangerous dogs, welfare scroungers, refugees and asylum seekers, and knife crime.

Questions
1. How might media reporting of an increase in knife crime cause deviance amplification?
2. How might the media report the problem without causing amplification?

Changing public concerns and attitudes

As the mods and rockers case shows, media representations of certain groups can change public attitudes by triggering a moral panic. Media portrayals of the mods and rockers as folk devils led to anxiety among the public that youths were out of control and posed a threat to society.

Since the Islamist terrorist attacks on the United States in 2001, media reporting of Islam and Muslims has been largely negative, as Box 3 shows. This has contributed to a change in public attitudes and especially a rise in Islamophobia in the general population. This may account for the rise in hate crimes against Muslims seen in recent years.

Box 3   Newspaper reporting of Muslims

Analysis of 143 million words of British newspaper articles by Paul Baker et al showed an overwhelmingly negative portrayal of Muslims and Islam. They found the following.

Islam and Muslims were often reported using words such as threat, fundamentalism, terrorist, extremist and sexist. The words 'Muslim' and 'Islamic' were often linked with words denoting violence (e.g. 'Islamic terrorism', 'Muslim fanatics').

The term 'the Muslim community' was used to portray Muslims as a homogeneous group (all the same), in conflict with the UK and containing dangerous radical elements. The term often appeared alongside words such as anger, fear, warning, criticism, unrest, outrage, offensive and antagonising. The term helped to create the idea of Muslims as belonging to a separate group and contributed towards a process of 'othering'.

Newspapers often used police mugshots to portray Muslims. Stories focusing on extremism increased over time, whereas stories focusing on attacks on Muslims decreased.

Newspapers also print letters from readers and articles by columnists with extremely negative views of Muslims. This allows the paper to distance itself from such views while still giving them exposure.

Perceptions of crime trends

Is crime increasing, decreasing or staying the same? Are particular types of crime becoming more or less frequent? In general, the public seem more likely to believe crime is on the increase. For example, the Crime Survey for England and Wales found that during 72% of people thought crime nationally had gone up, while 43% thought crime locally had increased.

The effect of the media

This difference between the national and local figures is significant. We have first-hand knowledge of our own area, but we rely on the media to tell us what is going on nationally. And as we saw in Topic 1.4, the media give a lot of coverage to crime, especially violent crime, and the tabloids often report it in highly sensationalised and alarmist ways. This gives the impression that there is a great deal of crime and that the problem is growing.

Fear of crime

One impact of the perception that crime is rising is an increased fear of becoming a victim. This can be caused by the media over-reporting certain types of crime, such as street robberies and violent and sexual attacks, portraying the typical victim as old and/or female. As a result, women and the elderly are more likely to fear becoming victims of crime on the streets. Yet in reality it is young males who are most at risk of being victims of violence outside the home.

Likewise, over-reporting of crimes against children, such as abductions and sexual abuse or violence by paedophiles, may make parents fearful of allowing their children to go out unsupervised. Again, however, children are more at risk of harm from family members than from strangers.

Research by Schlesinger and Tumber has also shown that tabloid readers and heavy users of TV have greater fear of becoming a victim of crime. This may be because of their greater exposure to media representations of such crimes.

However, in some cases people's perception of increased crime is accurate. Some local areas have rising crime rates and residents may have been victims or know friends or neighbours who have been victims. In this case, their fear may be based on personal experience rather than media representations.

Stereotyping of criminals

A stereotype is an oversimplified generalisation or label applied a whole group of people; for example, 'all young people are lazy'. Stereotyping can play a major part in which types of people attract the attention of the criminal justice system.

Typifications

According to Aaron Cicourel, the police, judges, probation officers and prosecutors have stereotypes of 'the typical delinquent'. Cicourel calls these 'typifications'. He found that police officers saw the typical delinquent as having characteristics such as the following:

- young, lower-class males, often unemployed
- often Black or minority ethnic background
- from a 'rough' neighbourhood
- with a 'bad attitude' to authority
- a poor educational record, truanting etc.
- associating with others known to the police.

It is likely that the police get their typifications in part from the media: media portrayals of offenders are often similar to the police typifications that Cicourel describes. For example, local TV news reports and 'reality TV' shows often show young working-class males as offenders and run-down neighbourhoods or council housing estates as scenes of crime.

Self-fulfilling prophecy

The police use these typifications to make decisions about where to patrol, who to stop and question, whether to arrest or charge someone and so on. This can create a self-fulfilling prophecy: people who fit the typification are more likely to be caught when they do something wrong because police are on the lookout for such 'types'. They then get convicted and this confirms to officers that they need to watch out for these 'types' in future, leading to further arrests.

Meanwhile, offenders who don't fit the typification are more likely to be ignored by the police and get away with their offences. This helps to explain why seemingly 'respectable' white collar criminals may go unpunished.

Like the police, the public too form stereotypes based on media portrayals of 'the typical criminal'. As a result, they may be sensitised to any misbehaviour by groups such as young, Black, working-class, inner-city males, and therefore more likely to report the matter to the police.

ACTIVITY / Discussion

Stereotyping of criminals   Go to www.criminology.uk.net

Levels of response to crime and types of punishment

The media can affect the levels of response to crime by the police and the punishment handed out by the courts. We can look at two examples of this: the mods and rockers, and the riots of 2011.

Mods and rockers

The media's sensational reporting of events and their demonising of young people as folk devils included calls for the police and courts to crack down.

For example, Cohen documents cases of police making arbitrary arrests before any offence had been committed, arresting innocent bystanders, and provoking people into committing offences (for example by pushing them around until they reacted). Similarly, the courts remanded defendants in prison for trivial offences, and sentences for those convicted were unusually harsh. This was partly because magistrates felt it necessary to 'teach them a lesson' and partly to set an example that would deter others from similar behaviour.

The 2011 riots

The riots began following a demonstration outside Tottenham police station to protest at the shooting to death of Mark Duggan by Metropolitan Police officers. Rioting quickly spread to other parts of the country.

According to Simon Rogers, the sentences imposed on those convicted of offences committed during the riots were disproportionately harsh. For example:

- **Youth courts** gave custodial sentences to 32% of those convicted, compared with only 5% for those convicted of similar offences in 2010 (the year before the riots).
- **Magistrates' courts** sent 37% of those convicted to jail, compared with only 12% for similar cases in 2010, and the average sentence was almost three times as long.
- **Crown courts** sent 82% of those convicted to jail, compared with only 33% of similar cases in 2010. Sentences were eight months longer on average.

Commenting on such sentences, the former chair of the Criminal Bar Association, Paul Mendelle QC, said there is a danger that the courts may get caught up in a "kind of collective hysteria and actually go over the top and hand out sentences which are too long and too harsh."

The London riots, August 2011. Firefighters and police attend a burning building in Croydon.

The media's role

The media played a major part in setting the tone for the harsher sentences. For example, the *Daily Mail* described the rioters as 'illiterate and innumerate', engaged in an 'orgy' of looting and as 'wild beasts' who 'respond only to instinctive animal impulses — to eat and drink, have sex, seize or destroy the property of others.'

At the same time, most of the media made little attempt to examine the underlying causes of the riots. The media were also accused of being uncritical of the police's role in the death of Mark Duggan and their handling of the protest demonstration.

Questions

1. Why do you think the sentences for rioters in 2011 were severe?
2. Why would the media focus on the riots and rioters rather than the causes of the riots?

Moral entrepreneurs

We saw earlier that moral panics feature calls for a 'crackdown' on the folk devils involved. These calls are often led by what Howard Becker calls 'moral entrepreneurs'.

Moral entrepreneurs are individuals or pressure groups who lead a campaign or 'crusade' about a moral issue – for example about alcohol, pornography, drug-taking, abortion, mods and rockers, or homosexuality. They claim that the issue is a serious social problem and needs immediate action to tackle it. Moral entrepreneurs make great use of the media to call for a crackdown on the problem, for example demanding increased policing, harsher sentences, tighter laws and so on.

Moral entrepreneurs often come from the higher classes. They frequently include politicians, senior police officers and judges, and experts and professionals of various kinds. In the case of both the mods and rockers and the 2011 riots, moral entrepreneurs were often quoted, interviewed or provided with air time and newspaper space to give their diagnoses, predictions and solutions to the problems.

ACTIVITY / Media

Riots   Go to www.criminology.uk.net

Changing priorities and emphasis

When the media voice concern about a particular type of crime or anti-social behaviour, it may lead to changes in the priorities or policies of government, the police and other agencies. It may even lead to new laws being introduced. Two examples of changes in priorities that led to changes in the law are the issues of dangerous dogs, and illegal raves.

Dangerous dogs

In 1990 and 1991, the tabloid newspapers carried reports on Rottweilers and pit bull terriers that had mauled and in some cases killed children. The language used was sensational and emotive: typical headlines included 'Savaged' and 'Muzzle these devils'. Coverage also included gory photographs of the victims.

Media coverage labelling pit bulls as 'devil dogs' encouraged the view that they posed a widespread and serious threat. This led to calls for something to be done and criticisms of the lack of action from John Major's Conservative government. As a result, the Home Secretary Kenneth Baker felt it necessary to push emergency legislation through Parliament. The Dangerous Dogs Act (DDA) became law in August 1991.

The DDA made it illegal to own, breed or sell pit bulls and three other breeds. Dogs found to be illegal would be destroyed and the owner could be jailed for up to six months.

Politics Another factor causing the change in the government's priorities was the political situation at the time. Baker had been severely criticised for his handling of prison riots in the previous year. By responding quickly to media and public demands he could show that he was a 'man of action', so a quick 'win' with a popular policy looked very attractive.

Criticisms of the DDA

The DDA has been widely criticised as a knee-jerk over-reaction to tabloid headlines. One critic describes it as 'a classic example of what not to do'.

The DDA was a response to a moral panic that exaggerated the dangers. Deaths caused by dog attacks are actually very rare: there were only 30 deaths in the first 25 years after the DDA was passed, and 21 of these were caused by dogs not covered by the Act.

'Blame the deed, not the breed'

One problem with the DDA is in deciding whether a dog is a pit bull or not. Critics also argue that destroying dogs just because of their breed is a form of 'doggy genocide'. They claim we should 'blame the deed, not the breed' and that the law should target irresponsible owners, not the dogs.

Dog lovers protest against breed specific legislation for so-called dangerous dogs.

In fact, as Baker admitted, there are more reported dog bites by some other breeds than by pit bulls, but if he had put dogs such as Alsatians and Dobermans into the same category, it "would have infuriated the 'green welly' brigade" of middle- and upper-class Conservative voters.

Critics such as Lodge and Hood argue that there is a 'canine class issue' here. Pit bull owners have been labelled and stigmatised by the media as irresponsible, lower-class 'chavs' living on council estates. The dogs themselves have been portrayed as a macho status symbol favoured by gang members and drug dealers.

Illegal raves

The media also played a major part in changing government and police priorities in relation to illegal raves. 'Rave culture' first emerged in the late 1980s, characterised by taking the drug Ecstasy (MDMA) and dancing to acid house music at 'raves' often held at venues in rural areas.

Media reaction Initial media reaction was fairly favourable, with the *Sun* selling 'smiley face' T-shirts and describing acid house as 'groovy and cool'. However, the first signs of a moral panic began to emerge in 1988, with the *Sun* warning:

> "You will hallucinate. For example, if you don't like spiders you'll start seeing giant ones. There's a good chance you'll end up in a mental hospital for life. There's a good chance you'll be sexually assaulted while under the influence. You may not even know it until a few days or weeks later."

BBC documentaries made exaggerated claims about the dangers of Ecstasy. According to Sam Bradpiece, the BBC repeatedly demonised rave culture as a threat to society, justifying a tough response from government and the law.

Change in the law Finally the government changed the law specifically to stop raves. The 1994 Criminal Justice and Public Order Act applies to open-air gatherings of 100 or more people where amplified music with repetitive beats is played at night and is likely to cause distress to local residents. (This is the only time a particular style of music has ever been made illegal.) Those attending the rave can be arrested without a warrant.

Politics As well as the role of the media in changing priorities in the law, politics also played a part. The hedonistic (pleasure-seeking) culture of the rave scene was sharply opposed to the values of the Conservative governments of Margaret Thatcher and John Major, which emphasised self-discipline, hard work and individualism.

CONTROLLED ASSESSMENT PREPARATION

What you have to do

Using your notes from Topic 1.5 *Explain the impact of media representations on the public perception of crime*, give a clear and detailed explanation of the impact of a range of media representations on the public perception of crime.

Impact

- moral panic
- changing public concerns and attitudes
- perceptions of crime trends
- stereotyping of criminals
- levels of response to crime and types of punishment
- changing priorities and emphasis.

You should be familiar with specific examples of media portrayal of criminality and the range of impacts given. Understanding of those impacts should be based on theories.

The assignment brief scenario

Where relevant you should make reference to the brief in your answer.

How it will be marked

4-6 marks: Clear and detailed explanation of the impact of a range of media representations on the public perception of crime.
1-3 marks: Limited explanation of the impact of media representations on the public perception of crime.

Evaluate methods of collecting statistics about crime

Getting started

You have been asked to write a report about levels of crime in your local area.

In small groups:

1. What sources might you use to obtain information about crime levels in the area?

2. What would be the advantages or disadvantages of these sources?

Two sources of crime statistics

How much crime is there, and how do we know? What can crime statistics tell us?

Criminologists have two main sources of statistics on crime:

- Home Office statistics – police recorded crime
- The Crime Survey for England and Wales (CSEW) – a survey of victims of crime.

In this Topic, we shall examine these two sources of crime statistics and evaluate their usefulness.

Home Office statistics: police recorded crime

The UK has 43 regional police forces plus the British Transport Police. Every month, each force reports to the Home Office the number of crimes they have recorded in their area. These figures are sent on to the Office for National Statistics, who publish final statistics for the whole country.

The statistics cover all notifiable offences – that is, all crimes that could be tried by a jury, plus some less serious crimes that are tried by a magistrate, such as assault without injury.

In addition to the national crime statistics, each police force publishes statistics for its area. You can also find crime statistics and crime maps for your local area online.

Reliability

Reliability refers to whether a method for collecting information about something gives the same result if used by a different person. If a method is reliable, then when it is repeated by someone else, it gives the same consistent result.

Strength Police recorded crime statistics are generally thought of as reliable because different officers and different police forces classifying a given incident would be expected to follow the same procedures, use the same definitions of crimes and so on.

Limitations However, it is still possible for different officers to classify the same incident differently. For example, if a victim had suffered only a couple of minor scratches in an attack, one officer might classify this as assault without injury while another might decide it was assault with injury.

Likewise, different forces may define a crime differently. For example, one force might have a policy of not recording thefts of property worth less than £10, while another might have a threshold of £20 – so when we compare their theft statistics, we are not comparing like with like.

Validity

Validity refers to whether the statistics give us a true picture of the amount of crime. Police recorded crime statistics may not do so. For example, the police recorded over 55,000 rapes in 2019-2020, but this understates the true number, both because many victims do not report the offence and because the police may fail to record it.

Recorded crime figures do not include:

- Crimes that have not been reported to the police: according to the CSEW, people only report about 40% of the crimes they have been victims of.

- Incidents that the police decide not to record as crimes. They only record about 60% of the crimes that people report to them.

Reasons for under-reporting

For a crime to be reported, a victim or witness must first of all believe a crime has occurred. For example, you may not notice an item has gone missing, or you may think you lost it rather than that someone has stolen it.

Why do only 1 in 4 rapes and attempted rapes get reported to the police?

Even if you believe a crime has occurred, there are many reasons why you may not report it:

- If a stolen item was of low value or uninsured: e.g. cars are often high value and most are insured, so car thefts generally do get reported.

- You may have no faith in the police: you may see them as incompetent or unhelpful.

- You may feel embarrassed or ashamed: e.g. because you failed to take sensible precautions to avoid being a victim.

- Fear of reprisals from the offender.

- You may prefer to deal with it yourself: e.g. if a relative steals from you, you may not want to get them in trouble with the police.

- You may fear getting into trouble yourself: e.g. if you have been illegally trafficked, you may not want to report that you have been abused.

ACTIVITY / Discussion

Reasons for under-reporting crime   Go to www.criminology.uk.net

---

Reasons for under-recording

Once a crime is reported, the police must decide whether or not to record it. Police have some discretion about whether to record a crime and may choose not to do so for several reasons:

- They may not believe the victim's story.

- They may not have enough evidence to secure a conviction.

- The victim may refuse to press charges.

For example, they may have had a more traumatic experience of crime. If so, the final results may not be fully representative of the population. Also, although the sample is large, it may not be big enough to give a representative picture of less frequent but very serious crimes.

ACTIVITY / **Discussion**

Crime surveys · Go to www.criminology.uk.net

Differences between crime levels according to different sources

The CSEW consistently records more crimes than the police statistics and sometimes the two measures of crime give different pictures of whether it is increasing or decreasing. The differences between the two are mainly due to differences in reporting – the CSEW is able to capture crime that goes unreported to the police.

Which measure is more useful?

Despite its shortcomings such as not including certain crimes and certain victims, the CSEW is the more useful of the two measures of crime. As we have seen, the Office for National Statistics (ONS) decided that police recorded crime statistics do not come up to the required standard for UK government statistics. As John Flatley of the ONS has said, the CSEW 'remains our best guide to long-term trends for crime as experienced by the population in general'.

| Box 5 | Other sources of crime statistics |

Apart from the CSEW and Home Office statistics, there are other sources of crime statistics.

Statistics on convicted criminals One problem with these statistics is that they only tell us about people who have been found guilty – in other words, those who were too incompetent or unlucky to avoid being caught – so they only measure how many *failed* criminals there are. They may be unrepresentative of the ones who got away.

Self-report studies ask people what crimes they have committed. They are conducted by confidential and anonymous questionnaires or interviews, so there are no major ethical issues. Anonymity also helps to ensure that people answer truthfully. They are useful in uncovering 'victimless' crimes such as drug use and those that are unlikely to be detected, such as fraud.

One finding of self-report studies is that there is little difference between the social classes or ethnic groups in their levels of offending. This may mean that the lower classes and Black people (who feature more in the official statistics) may just be more likely to be *convicted* of offences, rather than more likely to *commit* them. This could be due to labelling by the criminal justice system (see Topic 1.5).

However, respondents may not be completely truthful. Some may fear incriminating themselves, while others (young males, perhaps) may boast of crimes they haven't actually committed. However, evidence suggests that about 80% of respondents tell the truth. A further problem is that self-report studies don't generally ask about more serious crimes. If they did, answers might be less truthful.

Crimes against businesses The Commercial Victimisation Survey looks at crimes against businesses such as online crimes, burglary, vandalism, theft, robbery and assaults on staff. This fills a gap left by the CSEW, which only covers crimes against residents of households.

CONTROLLED ASSESSMENT PREPARATION

What you have to do

Using your notes from Topic 1.6 *Evaluate methods of collecting statistics about crime*, evaluate Home Office statistics and the Crime Survey for England and Wales as sources of information about crime.

Use the following criteria in your evaluation:

- reliability
- validity
- ethics of research
- strengths and limitations
- purpose of research.

How it will be marked

4-6 marks: Clear and detailed evaluation of two methods/sources of information used to collect information about crime with clear evidence of reasoning. Detailed and relevant reference to specific sources.

1-3 marks: Limited (may only list methods/sources of information) evaluation of methods of collecting information about crime.

Compare campaigns for change

Getting started

Working in small groups

1. Make a list of any campaigns for change you are aware of. These can be on any topic and do not need to focus on crime.

2. What is the purpose of the campaign? What does it want to change and why?

3. What information does the campaign give you?

4. How did you hear about the campaign?

5. Compare your answers with the rest of the class. Are there any similarities between the campaigns?

Campaigns for change

Members of society may want to bring about a change of some kind. They can do this by getting others to agree with what they want. This may be done by campaigning on an issue. In this Topic, we examine the purposes of campaigns for change.

Box 6	Policies and laws

Campaigns for change often aim to change laws and/or policies.

Policies are the plans and actions of government departments and agencies, such as the police and courts, schools and colleges, the welfare system, the NHS, social services, local authorities and other public bodies.

Laws Policies are usually based on laws introduced by government and passed by Parliament. Laws provide the framework within which government agencies operate. They set out the standards, procedures and principles that government agencies must follow to carry out the government's policies. For example, the law lays down the circumstances under which the police can legally carry out a stop and search policy.

Campaigns to change a policy

Some campaigns for change are focused on changing policies. These campaigns will often be directed at political parties and at the government, but also at other organisations. By influencing the view of political parties, campaigners will hope to bring about change more quickly.

An example: Unlock

One example of an organisation campaigning to bring about a change in policy is Unlock. Unlock was set up to help people who have a criminal conviction. Unlock is a charity that provides a voice and support for people with criminal convictions who are facing disadvantages because of their criminal record. Unlock has two goals:

- To help ex-offenders move on with their lives by empowering them with information, advice and support to overcome the stigma of their previous convictions.
- To promote a fairer and more inclusive society by challenging discriminatory practices against those with convictions and by promoting socially just alternatives.

A key approach of Unlock is 'ear to the ground, voice at the top', meaning that it listens to those needing change, while working with those who are able to bring about that change.

A major aim of Unlock is to change policies that limit the opportunities for people with a criminal record, for example in employment. Although there are laws preventing people with certain kinds of conviction from taking up jobs such as working with children, this is not true for most occupations. In most cases, it is at the employer's discretion whether to take on someone with a criminal conviction, yet many refuse to employ ex-offenders. Unlock campaigns to persuade employers to change their policies and employ individuals who have a conviction.

Campaigning methods

Unlock uses a wide range of campaigning methods, including the following:

- It has a website and blog which can be accessed by the public and where people can sign up to receive its newsletter.
- It makes media appearances to publicise its campaigns.
- It carries out and publishes research in areas of concern for those with criminal convictions.

Unlock's successes

Unlock has had many successes in changing policy in relation to offenders. In 2005, Unlock identified the problem of people coming out of prison who had managed to get jobs, but were losing these opportunities because they didn't have a bank account to get their wages paid into. Unlock campaigned for 9 years working with prisons and banks.

By 2014, nearly 6,000 bank accounts had been opened for people in prison, ready for them to use once they were released. 114 prisons now have links with a high-street bank. All prisons that wanted a bank account opening programme had one in place by the end of the project.

Campaigns to change the law

Some campaigns are aimed at changing an existing law because campaigners feel there is some problem with it. Other campaigns aim to introduce a new law in an area of public concern.

An example: Sarah's Law

An example of a campaign to achieve a change in the law was the successful campaign for 'Sarah's Law'. Sarah's Law allows people to ask police if a person who has access to a specific child has convictions for child sex offences. The new law was partly the result of a successful campaign by Sarah's mother, Sara Payne.

The background

The campaign to introduce Sarah's Law came as a result of the abduction and murder of eight-year-old Sarah Payne in 2000. Sarah was killed by a previously convicted paedophile who lived in the area. The campaign was started by Sarah's mother, who wanted to raise awareness of the fact that those with convictions for crimes against children could be living in an area without the knowledge of parents. Her campaign focused on changing the law so that parents would be able to have access to details of anyone living in their area who had a conviction for crimes against children.

The campaign for Sarah's Law followed a similar campaign in America in the 1990s to introduce Megan's Law, which had been successful in changing legislation to allow the public knowledge of convicted sex offenders in their area.

Media support

Key to Sara's campaign was support from the *News of the World*, a tabloid newspaper. In July 2000, the paper published the names and photographs of fifty people it claimed had committed child sex offences and pledged to carry on until it had 'named and shamed' every paedophile in Britain.

The *News of the World* publicising the campaign and the resulting actions from the 'name and shame' campaign increased the profile of Sara's campaign.

Success

The campaign's success can be seen from the implementation of the Child Sex Offender Disclosure Scheme, or Sarah's Law, across England and Wales; a similar scheme operates in Scotland. Sarah's Law allows anyone to ask police if someone in contact with a child has a record of child sexual offences. Police forces process the application, but disclosure is not guaranteed. There does not need to be a suspicion to have a check made on a person. Although anyone with an interest can use the scheme, it is most commonly used by parents and guardians.

Other campaigns to change the law include the following:

- **Dignity in Dying** campaigns to make it legal to choose the option of assisted dying for terminally ill, mentally competent adults. Currently, assisting a suicide is a crime with a maximum penalty of 14 years in prison.
- **Smoking in cars** The British Lung Foundation (BLF) ran a campaign to ban smoking in cars with children in them. BLF estimates that 430,000 children a week are exposed to cigarette smoke in cars. As a result of the campaign, the law was changed in 2015. If a person smokes in a car with children in it, both the smoker and the driver can be fined £50.

Sara Payne speaking at the Police Federation Conference. Using media support, she gained widespread backing for her campaign.

Campaigns to change the priorities of agencies

An agency is a governmental or private organisation that provides a service. In relation to crime and justice, this could refer for example to the police, the courts, the probation service or victim support. It can also refer to other agencies such as schools and colleges who may be able to influence those likely to offend.

An Example: No Knives, Better Lives

The priorities of agencies may change as a result of pressure from specific campaigns. One campaign to change priorities is 'No Knives, Better Lives' (NKBL), a national campaign to combat knife crime among young people in Scotland. It is run by YouthLink Scotland and the Scottish Government. NKBL works with local organisations to provide information and support. It seeks to draw attention to the consequences of carrying a knife.

Educational agencies NKBL's campaign focuses on schools and colleges, seeking to change their priorities so that they see it as part of their role to help reduce knife crime. The aim is to turn educational institutions into agencies that can work with those in danger of becoming involved in knife crime.

With this aim in mind, NKBL engages in a range of activities:

- It produces educational materials for schools to teach children about knife crime and its impact.
- Its website has a range of case studies highlighting the impact of knife crime.
- It has produced a series of videos to help educate young people about knife crime.
- There are blogs students and teachers can follow that provide information on knife crime and the work of NKBL.
- It recruits and trains peer educators – young people who work to raise awareness of the risks and consequences of carrying a knife.

NKBL has been successful in changing the priorities of schools and colleges so that they now see it as their responsibility to play a proactive role in reducing knife crime in Scotland.

Campaigns to achieve a change in funding

The purpose of some campaigns is to ensure adequate funding for their particular cause. This can involve finding ways to raise extra funds, for example by stepping up appeals to the public to make donations.

It can also involve finding ways to put the funding on a more secure or long term basis. For example, a campaign may seek to shift the source of its funds from just relying on public donations to instead persuading local or national government to fund its aims.

An example: #WeWontWait

A good example of a campaign to achieve a change in funding is #WeWontWait by Parkinson's UK. It aims to persuade the government and the NHS to commit more funds for research into Parkinson's disease, rather than much of this research having to be funded from public donations. At the same time, however, Parkinson's UK also campaigns for increased financial support from members of the public.

All-party support Parkinson's UK has support from the All-Party Parliamentary Group on Parkinson's disease, through which it lobbies government. This is a group of MPs and members of the House of Lords who work to keep the disease on the political agenda and to push for funding for new treatments and for care.

The campaign produces videos to highlight the nature of Parkinson's disease and runs Parkinson's Awareness Week. Sufferers are encouraged to make their own videos to highlight personal experiences of the disease to raise public awareness. The campaign also uses the hashtag #WeWontWait on Twitter to raise awareness of the need for funding.

Campaigns to change awareness

Many campaigns have the aim of changing the public's awareness of an issue or crime. This may mean that a campaign tries to help the public to better understand particular types of crime. A goal of campaigns that raise awareness may be:

- to encourage the public to help reduce crime
- to encourage victims of crime to come forward.

An example: #MeToo

The phrase 'me too' was used by Tarana Burke, a social activist, in 2006. It was part of a campaign in America on Myspace social media seeking to 'empower through empathy' – that is, to make women stronger by sharing and understanding each other's feelings. Originally, the campaign was aimed at poor Black women who had suffered sexual abuse. Burke used the phrase 'me too' because when she was confronted with a girl who had been abused, she wished she had said 'me too'.

The #MeToo campaign against sexual harassment and sexual assault was launched in 2017. It resulted from the highly publicised case of the film producer Harvey Weinstein and the multiple allegations of sexual abuse and misconduct made against him. This campaign uses the original 2006 slogan and asks women who have been victims of sexual harassment or abuse to tweet with the hashtag #MeToo.

The campaign aims to empower women and girls to come forward if they have been victims of sexual harassment, abuse or misconduct, for example in the workplace. The idea is to show the scale of abuse suffered by women.

The #MeToo movement has changed awareness of sexual assault and harassment.

Success

The campaign has succeeded in raising public awareness of the extent of the problem and the need for action to deal with it. Its success has been seen through the huge volume of tweets from women using the hashtag. On Facebook, #MeToo was used by more than 4.7 million people in the first 24 hours.

Although #MeToo began as a campaign for women to raise awareness of their experiences of sexual abuse, men also began tweeting and using the hashtag to show solidarity with the women and also tweeting their own experiences of abuse.

Campaigns to change attitudes

Changes in attitude are often a key purpose of a campaign. In some cases, this may be to help the public to accept and understand the problems caused by certain types of crime.

An example: Stop Hate UK

Stop Hate UK is a national organisation that campaigns to prevent hate crimes such as racist and homophobic attacks, and to encourage victims to report cases. It offers advice and support for victims and witnesses, and training to help overcome hate crime. Stop Hate UK works with the Crown Prosecution Service to help promote the reporting of hate crimes.

A key aim of the campaign is to change the attitudes of both victims and witnesses of hate crime towards reporting. The campaign encourages reporting of all forms of hate crime and offers guidance on what actions should be reported and the ways in which they can be reported. The campaign focuses on making people more willing to see hate crime as a problem and to recognise the consequences for its victims.

Stop Hate UK uses both Facebook and Twitter and regularly tweets relevant news in the field of hate crime. It also organises local events to promote its work and to make members of the public more aware of hate crime and its impact.

Success

A major success for the Stop Hate UK campaign has been the development of an app to enable the reporting of hate crime. The app means users in West Yorkshire can report crime in real time, whether they are a victim or a witness. It also allows users to include video or photographic evidence to support their report, while GPS shows where the crime is taking place.

Download our West Yorkshire **Hate Crime Reporting App.**

Download on the App Store — GET IT ON Google Play

Search for **Stop Hate UK**

The app allows real time reporting of hate crimes.

ACTIVITY / Research

Comparing campaigns   Go to www.criminology.uk.net

CONTROLLED ASSESSMENT PREPARATION

What you have to do

Using your notes and research from Topic 2.1 *Compare campaigns for change*, make clear and detailed comparisons of a range of relevant campaigns for change. Make explicit links to planned campaigns with reference to specific and appropriate sources to support conclusions.

You may choose from the following criteria in comparisons:

- change in policy
- change in law
- change in priorities of agencies
- change in funding
- change in awareness
- change in attitude.

You should:

- be aware that campaigns for change may have different purposes.
- compare examples of campaigns for change and examine their effectiveness in achieving their objectives.

How it will be marked

8-10 marks: Clear and detailed comparison of a range of relevant campaigns for change. Explicit links to planned campaign with reference to specific and appropriate sources to support conclusions.
4-7 marks: Some comparison of a range of campaigns for change. There are some links to planned campaigns to support decision making.
1-3 marks: Limited awareness of campaigns for change. Evidence is mainly descriptive.

Evaluate the effectiveness of media used in campaigns for change

Getting started

With a partner, answer the following.

1. Of the campaigns for change that you studied in the previous Topic, which one did you think was the best? Give reasons for your answer.

2. What do you think are the most effective ways of a campaign spreading its message and gaining support? Give reasons for your answer.

How campaigns use the media to bring about change

As we saw in the previous Topic, campaigns use a range of methods to promote their messages. In this Topic we will look at a range of different media used by campaigns to bring about change and we will evaluate their effectiveness.

Blogs

Blogs (short for web logs) usually contain information or discussions. People write blogs on a wide range of topics. Blogs are produced by businesses, media groups and campaigns, as well as by individuals.

Advantages Blogs are easy to create and cost little or nothing to set up. They provide an effective way of presenting a wide range of news, views and often detailed information about a campaign. Blogs often include links to social media pages, websites, video and other documents providing further information of relevance to the campaign's supporters.

An example: Unlock

Unlock, the organisation that campaigns to help people with a criminal conviction (see Topic 2.1), uses a blog to promote its work. The blog acts as a form of diary, giving regular in-depth updates on the progress of current campaigns. This is particularly useful for people who are already aware of Unlock and want to keep up with the latest developments.

Campaign directors can provide information directly to anyone who accesses the website via Unlock's blog. The blog also contains links to sources of information relevant to the work of the campaign, which is also of value to anyone carrying out research on the treatment of convicted offenders.

Disadvantages People who are not already aware of and interested in a campaign may be unlikely to access its blog. This means that a blog is unlikely to increase support for the campaign. The blog's in-depth nature makes it less accessible to people who just want some basic information about a campaign. In addition, blogs are not accessible to those without online access or those who are less confident with the technology. Blogs need to be kept up to date and this can be very time-consuming.

ACTIVITY / Research

Using blogs in campaigns   Go to www.criminology.uk.net

Viral messaging

Viral messaging involves passing messages from person to person via social media. One person may spread the message to many others, who in turn spread it further and so on.

Advantages Viral messaging is a cheap and potentially very effective way of spreading a campaign message widely. If a message 'goes viral', it can reach thousands or even millions of people extremely quickly – for example, when people re-tweet Twitter messages to their friends.

Disadvantages There is no guarantee that people will in fact pass on the message. To go viral, it must contain something that recipients identify with and feel inclined to share with members of their network – so the method is only as good as the message it is aiming to spread.

One way to increase the likelihood of the message going viral is by identifying individuals with 'high social networking potential' (SNP). This is related to the size of a person's social media network and their ability to influence others. A high SNP means the materials sent to the original recipient are more likely to reach others. However, it may not be easy to identify people with a high SNP.

Completing the activity below will help you evaluate the strengths and limitations of using viral messaging in a campaign.

ACTIVITY / **Using viral messaging in campaigns**

Send a message on social media to a group of friends. In the message you need to encourage them to pass the message to other friends and let you know how many friends they have forwarded it to.

See how quickly your message spreads.

Compare the class results. What do they tell you about the usefulness of social media in spreading messages?

Social networking

In 2020, 3.81 billion people worldwide used social media. Most people and organisations have a social network presence, for example on Facebook and Twitter. Many people also have a presence on sites focused on job prospects, such as LinkedIn. Most of the campaigns we considered in Topic 2.1 have some form of social network presence.

Advantages Since the purpose of social networking sites is to connect people via audio, video and text, they can be very useful campaigning tools. Having a Facebook or Twitter account gives a campaign the opportunity to reach a wide audience. Posts and messages will automatically reach followers, and sharing or retweeting means the message can be quickly passed on to others who may also choose to follow the campaign.

For example, #MeToo, the social networking-based campaign against sexual assault and harassment, uses a Twitter hashtag to demonstrate support. Its hashtag was used by more than 4.7 million people in its first 24 hours. This shows how effective social networking can be in rapidly raising awareness of a campaign issue among huge numbers of people and at very little cost.

Disadvantages Although those who follow a campaign may see and even react to a message, they may not actively support the campaign. For instance, in the case of Stop Hate UK, which campaigns against hate crime, a follower may show support for the campaign on social media but still not report incidents of hate crime, whether as a victim or a witness. For this reason, social networking is useful as an awareness-raising tool but not necessarily as an action tool.

Also, social networks rely on technology and campaigns face the risk of their pages being hacked, and of supporters being aggressively trolled by opponents.

Advertising

Many campaigns use paid advertisements to get their message across. These may range from posters for small local campaigns to large national advertising campaigns in newspapers and magazines and on radio, television and cinema.

Other ways of advertising include billboards, hand delivered leaflets through people's letterboxes, flyers given out to passers-by, asking local shops to display your posters, advertising on buses and trains, and advertising on social media such as Facebook.

Advantages Advertising can enable a campaign to reach its audience. Unlike many other methods, it does not rely on members of the public having a prior interest in the campaign. For example, TV and radio adverts will broadcast to all viewers or listeners of a channel or station. For smaller campaigns, leaflets or displays in shops mean many residents of an area could be made aware of a campaign. Advertising can sometimes be quite cheap, for example in a local newspaper.

Disadvantages Although an advertisement may reach a wide audience, there is no guarantee that the public will pay attention and it may be ignored or soon forgotten. TV viewers may go and make a cup of tea while the adverts are on. Leaflets may be thrown away unread.

Advertising can also be costly and the amount and type of advertising a campaign can undertake will depend partly on the funding it has available. For example, to advertise on prime-time national TV can cost as much as £40,000 for a 30-second commercial. This is in addition to the cost of making the advertisement in the first place, which may be even more expensive.

Complete the activity below to help you assess the cost of advertising and to evaluate whether this is a useful method for a campaign.

ACTIVITY Research

Working with a partner
1. Contact a local newspaper and find out how much they charge for a half-page advertisement.
2. Contact a local radio station and ask them how much they charge for a 30-second advertisement.

Web banners

One way a campaign can use advertising is by producing a web banner. This is a form of advertising that asks supporters with a webpage to show their support for the campaign by pasting its banner onto their page. For example, Stop Hate UK invites supporters to use its web banner to promote National Hate Crime Awareness Week.

Advantages Web banners can reach large audiences if they are displayed on popular sites. Also, in contrast to most other forms of advertising, this is free.

Disadvantages The use of web banners relies on the good will of the campaign's supporters to display the advertising for free. It may be that only strong supporters of a campaign would be willing to permit a campaign to display its web banner on their webpage.

Merchandise

Another way to advertise is by selling merchandise linked to the campaign. A range of items can be sold, such as badges, T-shirts, wristbands and mugs.

Advantages Selling merchandise brings the double advantage of raising money for the campaign while at the same time spreading its message. Members of the public may be more willing to give money to a campaign if they get a product in return. Items carrying the campaign's logo or message mean that the user or wearer of the merchandise provides the campaign with free publicity.

Disadvantages Merchandise requires supporters to give money to the campaign. The campaign will also have to spend money to produce the merchandise in the first place and may not get it back if it cannot be sold.

Radio

Campaigns often use radio to promote their message and raise their profile with a wide audience. There are several possibilities for radio publicity. For example:

- Radio stations are often willing to interview campaign representatives on air about the campaign or invite them to contribute to phone-in debates and discussions.
- Similarly, they may invite members of campaign groups to speak as experts in their field to give their opinion on magazine and news programmes.

Local stations are likely to be more interested in campaigns with a local angle, whereas national radio stations are more likely to want campaigns with a wider appeal.

Advantages Radio interviews offer free publicity, without the expense of advertising. Speaking as an expert on a radio programme will highlight a campaign and the importance of supporting its aims.

Disadvantages If the presenter is hostile to the campaign they may show it in a negative light or seek to trip up the campaigner with their questioning. Programme makers may invite opponents of the campaign onto the show, or receive hostile calls during phone-ins. Campaigners may not have the knowledge or media skills to deal with this successfully.

Television

Campaigns may use television to promote their cause. As with radio, a local campaign might try to appear on a local news bulletin to get free exposure. Higher profile campaigns may aim for coverage on national news.

Advantages Appearances by campaign representatives on popular TV programmes can reach a wide audience and are a way to get the campaign's message across for free. Alternatively, television advertising can be used to convey the message using striking images, music, voice-overs or appeals from prominent supporters. Particular groups, such as teenagers, mothers or motorists, can be targeted by placing adverts in programmes that attract these groups. Alternatively a wider spread of the population can be reached by advertising in programmes such as the prime-time soap operas watched by millions.

Disadvantages As with radio, members of a campaign appearing on TV may encounter hostility from presenters or other guests on a programme that could undermine the message or show the campaign in a bad light. Also, TV advertising can be extremely expensive both to produce and to buy time on air, especially for prime-time broadcasting. Viewers may switch channels rather than watch adverts.

ACTIVITY Research

1. Watch a local or national TV news bulletin each day for two or three days. Make a note of any appearances by members of campaign groups. Make a note of the issue, the campaign and whether it was local or national.

2. When watching TV, make a note of any advertisements for campaigns.

3. Summarise your findings on the use of television by campaigns for change. Do you think appearances on the news were beneficial to the campaigns you saw? Give reasons for your answer.

Film

Films can be used to promote the campaign's message – whether on the cinema screen, on television, or online on YouTube or the campaign's own website. Campaigns can produce information films and videos, for example showing case studies of campaign issues. See also documentaries below.

Advantages Films can show a very positive view of a campaign. They can show visual images that may encourage people to support a campaign, for example by showing the difficulties faced by people.

An example

Parkinson's UK campaign uses films as a campaign tool. The organisation has its own YouTube channel and it invites sufferers to make films about living day-to-day with Parkinson's disease, which are then shown on the channel.

This approach gives a deeper insight into the disease for anyone considering supporting Parkinson's UK. The use of personal stories adds a human dimension to the illness and can act to encourage funding from both the government and the general public.

Disadvantages Depending on the nature of the campaign, the images may be too distressing for some viewers. Producing a film is also costly and, as with advertising, there is no guarantee that people will watch it.

ACTIVITY / Media

Campaign films   Go to www.criminology.uk.net

Documentary

Campaigns often use documentaries on TV, film or radio to promote their cause. Documentaries use images, audio, factual information, arguments and other material to provide a report or investigation about an issue. 'Docu-dramas' that mix factual reporting with reconstructions using actors are sometimes also used to portray real events for which no footage exists.

Advantages Presenting facts and arguments in visual or audio form can be a powerful way to promote a campaign. Documentaries can also be made showing the work of a campaign and its successes or aims.

Disadvantages Documentaries and docu-dramas can be costly to produce. As with film, a further limitation is being able to find an audience who will watch the production. Often this may only be those who are already committed to a campaign.

ACTIVITY / Media

Knife crime   Go to www.criminology.uk.net

Word of mouth

Campaign messages can be spread by word of mouth. Campaigners can 'get the ball rolling' by telling family and friends about the campaign. To spread the message more widely, campaigners may look to inform influencers and opinion leaders trusted by the campaign's target audience.

Advantages The great advantage of this method is that it costs nothing apart from time. Supporters are also likely to be eager to tell others about the campaign. Opinion leaders and influencers may increase support for the campaign by using their influence to bring others on board.

Disadvantages Word of mouth can be a slow process because it is largely a question of telling one person at a time. There is also a risk that the campaign's message may become garbled or distorted as it passes from person to person.

Questions

1. Make a list of the characteristics of the kind of person you would imagine as an opinion leader.
2. Who would you choose to act as an opinion leader for a campaign about hate crime? Give reasons for your answer.

Events

Events can take many forms; for example, it could be a family fun day to attract people of all ages, or a sporting event such as a football match. A celebrity such as a sports star or soap actor, or a prominent figure from the local community, can be invited to open the event.

Advantages Holding an event can be an effective way to launch a campaign and can be useful for focusing support. Events are a good opportunity to sign up supporters and to sell merchandise. Sponsored events such as fun runs can be used to raise campaign funds, while large-scale televised events can raise funds from viewers. Inviting a celebrity or a prominent figure from the local community can increase attendance at the event and help raise the campaign's profile, for example by attracting local press, TV or radio news coverage.

Disadvantages Events can be costly and time-consuming to organise and publicise. They may not be well attended if the publicity or activities are not appealing, or (in the case of outdoor events) if the weather is bad. The event will be competing with all the other things people may want or need to do at that time.

Questions

1. Imagine you are arranging an event to publicise a campaign. What kind of event would you choose?
2. Where would you hold the event? Give reasons to support your answer.

Print

Print media include local and national newspapers and magazines. There are two basic ways of gaining coverage for a campaign in newspapers and magazines:

- **paid advertisements**
- **press releases** – written communications sent to editors and journalists to announce something newsworthy in the hope that the newspaper will give it coverage.

Advantages Sending press releases to local or national papers can be a way of gaining free publicity for the campaign. For example, a campaign might want to promote a forthcoming event, publicise a recent success it has had or highlight a campaign issue using a human interest story. Well written press releases are very attractive to the press because they provide ready-made news articles.

An example Newspaper coverage can widen the exposure of a campaign because many people regularly buy a paper. For example, the News of The World, which backed the campaign to introduce Sarah's Law, had a circulation of over four million readers at the time. This meant the campaign's message reached a huge number of people. The emotive nature of the topic – the murder of a child – and the language the paper used motivated many to support the campaign.

Flyers are another way print can be used to spread a campaign's message. These can be distributed by campaigners relatively quickly and easily. Flyers can be designed to be eye-catching to increase support for a campaign.

Disadvantages Printing flyers or advertising in newspapers incurs a cost to the campaign, while writing effective press releases is a skill that not every campaigner has. Also, in a digital age, print media may be less appealing – newspaper sales have been in decline for many years. Young people especially are less likely to read newspapers and may prefer to access information online instead.

Complete the activity below to evaluate the use of local newspapers by a campaign.

ACTIVITY / **Research**

Find an example of a local campaign for change in your area that has been in the local newspaper. (The campaign doesn't have to be about crime.)

1. What was reported in the newspaper about the campaign?
2. What do you think the story achieved for the campaign? Did the story raise awareness of an issue? If so, in what way, such as use of a real-life case?
3. What facts and/or figures did the story contain?
4. Was the story designed to help raise funds for the campaign?
5. Summarise the advantages of using local newspapers in a campaign for change.

Websites

Most campaigns have a presence online. In addition to using social media sites, campaigns may develop their own websites. Often social media pages will have links to the campaign website.

Advantages Websites are easily accessible to potential supporters via a variety of different devices. Websites give campaigns the opportunity to present information in a format of their choosing. For example, No Knives, Better Lives has separate pages for parents, young people, and practitioners such as teachers. This enables different groups to access information relevant to their own particular needs or interests.

Disadvantages To be effective, a campaign's website needs members of the public to visit it, but without prior knowledge of the campaign, this is unlikely to happen. The website needs to be publicised, for example by using a web banner on other sites. The website also needs to be designed, created and maintained, which adds to its costs.

CONTROLLED ASSESSMENT PREPARATION

What you have to do

Using your notes and research from Topic 2.2 *Evaluate the effectiveness of media used in campaigns for change*, evaluate the effectiveness of the following media used in campaigns for change:

- blogs
- viral messaging
- social networking
- advertising
- radio
- television
- film
- documentary
- word of mouth
- events
- print.

You should have knowledge of the media and specific materials used in campaigns and be able to evaluate their effectiveness in promoting a campaign for change.

How it will be marked

11-15 marks: Clear and detailed evaluation of effectiveness of a range of media used in relevant campaigns for change. Clear evidence of well-reasoned judgements to support conclusions.

6-10 marks: Some evaluation of the effectiveness of a range of media used in relevant campaigns for change. Response is largely descriptive but includes some appropriate judgements.

1-5 marks: Limited evaluation of the effectiveness of media used in campaigns for change. Evidence is mainly descriptive and limited in range.

Plan a campaign for change relating to crime

Getting started

Working on your own

1. Make a list of five types of under-reported crime that a campaign could be based on.

2. From your list of types of crime, choose the one that you want to use for your campaign for change. Give reasons for your choice.

Important advice

As part of the controlled assessment, you must plan your own individual campaign. This Topic contains a series of activities designed to give you practice planning a campaign. It is essential that you complete all of these activities so that you will be properly prepared to tackle the controlled assessment.

Planning your practice campaign

This Topic deals with how to plan your practice campaign for change relating to crime. For this you will obviously need to choose a particular type of crime to focus on.

Which type of crime?

You should create a practice campaign for an under-reported or hidden crime. This could be a crime from among the ones covered in Topic 1.1. These are white collar crime, moral crime, state crime, technological crime and individual crime (including hate crime, 'honour' crime and domestic abuse).

What aspects do you need to address?

Whatever the type of crime, you will need to make decisions about the following:

- Your aims
- Your objectives
- Justifying your choice of practice campaign
- Your target audience
- Your methods and materials
- Finances
- Timescales
- Other resources you will need.

In this Topic, we shall examine each of these in turn and give you guidance on how to tackle them. When you have completed the Activities associated with these issues, you will have devised your practice campaign plan.

Your aims

The aim or aims of your practice campaign are what you hope it will achieve. Your campaign may have more than one aim, but don't have too many or you may lose focus.

You should focus your aims on one or more of the different purposes of campaigns that you studied in the previous Topic. We saw there that campaigns may aim to change a law or a policy, or the priorities of an agency. Similarly, they may seek to change funding, or to change people's awareness of an issue or their attitudes towards it. For example, your aim could be to change young people's awareness of the effects of knife crime.

Your campaign name Choose a suitable name for your practice campaign that reflects its aims.

ACTIVITY / Research

Types of change   Go to www.criminology.uk.net

Your aim(s) should be:

- **targeted**, identifying who or what needs to change
- **focused on impact**, spelling out what change the campaign will bring about
- **brief and clearly expressed.**

Your objectives

The objectives of your practice campaign are how you intend to meet your aims. Objectives are the stages or steps that you will carry out in producing your campaign. Each of your objectives should be SMART: specific, measurable, achievable, relevant and time-bound. Below is an example of one objective that you might need to achieve if you were running a campaign to raise young people's awareness of the dangers of carrying a knife.

SMART	Explanation	Example
Specific	Clear and to the point, not vague and general.	I will produce and distribute material that highlights the dangers of carrying a knife.
Measurable	You can track progress and easily see when you have reached each objective.	I will give out 1,000 leaflets to school students.
Achievable	Objectives must be something you are able to do.	I have permission from head teachers to hand out my leaflets.
Relevant	Your objectives should be closely linked to your aims. You should be able to explain how each one takes you closer to achieving your campaign aims. Do not have objectives that have nothing to do with what you hope to achieve.	This will reach my target audience of young people who may be at risk of carrying a knife or aware of others who do so.
Time-bound	This means you must have an idea of how long each objective will take and stick to that time frame.	I will distribute 200 leaflets per day for 5 days.

Table 1 SMART objectives

Linking your aims and objectives

There needs to be a clear link between the aims (*what* the campaign intends to achieve) and the objectives (*how* you intend to achieve those aims). However, the objectives should not just repeat the aims; they should be clear steps to achieve the aims.

ACTIVITY / **Linking your aims and objectives**

1. List the aim(s) of your practice campaign. Remember to include the type of crime and target audience, and make sure you include the purpose of your campaign.
2. Break down your aim(s) into a series of objectives that are SMART.

Justifying the campaign

As well as stating what you aim to do and how you intend to do it, you need to justify why you have chosen your practice campaign. The activity below will enable you to produce your justification for your choice of campaign.

ACTIVITY / Justifying the campaign

1. For your chosen type of crime, list all the reasons why this crime might not be reported. For example, there may be personal and/or social and cultural reasons for not reporting it.

2. What are the consequences of the lack of reporting of this crime? For example, does it affect police priorities, or lead to under-recording of the crime? Note all those that apply.

3. Note how this type of crime is portrayed in the media. For example, is it sensationalised or glamourised? What might be the impact of any reporting on public perceptions of this crime? For example, has the reporting created a moral panic about the crime?

4. Find police recorded crime statistics and statistics from the Crime Survey for England and Wales on the crime in your practice campaign. Do these highlight issues that justify your campaign? For example, is the crime under-recorded in the police statistics?

5. Look back at Topics 2.1 and 2.2 and note any features of previous campaigns for change that you would like to include in your practice campaign.

6. Note any real-life examples of the crime. These could be local examples, ones that have been in the news recently, or ones linked to campaigns you have studied.

Your target audience

Your practice campaign will be aimed at a particular group (or groups) of people; these are your target audience. Your aims should identify your target audience and your objectives should refer to the audience where appropriate.

You need to be able to explain why your audience is relevant to the campaign you have chosen. For example, it makes sense to aim a campaign about knife crime at young people, because they are more likely to be both victims and perpetrators of this type of crime.

ACTIVITY / Who is your target audience?

1. Identify the target audience for your practice campaign.

2. Do your aims and objectives refer to this group? If not, add the target audience to them.

3. Explain why your target audience are relevant. What is their connection to the type of crime you have chosen? For example, are they potential victims? Offenders? Witnesses? People who might prevent the crime?

4. Are there any key characteristics of your target audience that you need to consider when designing your practice campaign – for example, their age, gender or ethnicity?

Methods and materials

Your objectives will include details of the methods and materials you are going to use for your campaign. When planning your methods, you should refer to Topics 2.1 and 2.2 to help you choose which methods will be best for your aims and objectives.

Methods In choosing your methods, you need to make sure they fit with your target audience. For example, if your campaign was about young people and knife crime, you might choose to use social media to reach your audience, because young people are heavy users of social media.

Materials Similarly, your choice of materials also needs to consider your target audience. Explain how you will use your materials and why they will be relevant to your audience. For example, producing mugs might not be the best way to engage young people.

A poster with a striking image can be a very effective way of getting your anti-crime message across.

Finances

Your costs Finance is an essential part of almost any campaign. Your plan needs to consider what your campaign is going to cost. This will depend on your methods and materials and these will link to engaging your target audience.

You will need to make a realistic estimate of these costs. For example, if you intend to give away merchandise, you need to fully research the costs of that merchandise. If merchandise proves expensive you may choose to sell it during events or online to help recoup your costs.

Fundraising You need to consider how you will raise enough money to run your practice campaign. You will therefore need to include fundraising as part of your campaign plan. What you intend to spend cannot be more than the likely amount you will raise from your fundraising activities, so it's important that you make as realistic an estimate as possible of what you think you can raise. Don't be over-optimistic.

Timescales

This links to the time-bound element of your SMART objectives. To make the campaign a success, you need to ensure that everything is completed in good time. You should work out how much time you are going to need for each of the following stages:

- **Planning and research** This involves gathering information about the issue and formulating your aims and objectives.
- **Design** You will need to allocate time to choose or produce images and words for use in your campaign.
- **Materials** You need to allow time to create or obtain the campaign materials.
- **Implementation** Consider when you will launch your practice campaign and how long it will take to get the message out to your target audience.

ACTIVITY / Timescales

Using the bullet points above, formulate a timeframe for each stage of your practice campaign.

Other resources you will need

Finally, you should consider any further resources you may need for your campaign in addition to the materials you have already identified. For example, these resources could include:

- **Volunteers** You may need to recruit a team to help you, for example to run events, distribute leaflets, put up posters, collect donations or signatures for petitions.
- **Training** Those who are helping you may need training. For example, if you are holding an event to raise awareness about knife crime, volunteers may need training in how to communicate with young people, plus knowledge of the issues involved.

ACTIVITY / Research

Planning your practice campaign   Go to www.criminology.uk.net

CONTROLLED ASSESSMENT PREPARATION

In the controlled assessment you will need to produce campaign materials. You can practise this by producing materials for the campaign that you planned in Topic 3.1. However, although you can take your notes from this work into the controlled assessment, you will not be allowed to take in previously designed materials.

What you have to do

Using your notes and research from Topic 3.1 *Plan a campaign for change relating to crime*, you should identify an appropriate campaign for change. You should produce a detailed and comprehensive plan for your campaign, including clearly described actions in a relevant time sequence.

Your plan should include:

- aims and objectives
- justification of choice of campaign
- target audience
- methods to be used
- materials to be used
- finances
- timescales
- resources needed.

How it will be marked

8-10 marks: Detailed and appropriate plan for campaign, relevant to selected assignment brief, including clearly described actions in a relevant time sequence.

4-7 marks: Plan for campaign, relevant to selected assignment brief, has evidence of some appropriate actions in a relevant time sequence in some detail.

1-3 marks: Plan for campaign, relevant to selected assignment brief, is limited in detail. Appropriate actions, sequences and time are briefly outlined.

Design materials for use in campaigning for change

Getting started

1. Working in small groups, before you consider the design for your own practice campaign, look at some other campaigns to give you some ideas. Collect a range of publicity materials, such as leaflets or webpages, for any crime prevention campaigns you can find. These may be available online or from the police, libraries, community centres etc. Aim to get a range of campaigns to give you as many ideas as possible.

2. Working on your own, look for any posters and other public displays (e.g. on buses) that relate to crime prevention campaigns or campaigns for change. Take photographs so that you have a copy of these to refer to.

3. As a class, examine and discuss all the materials you have gathered to decide which ones have effective designs and why those designs are effective.

> **Important advice**
>
> As part of the controlled assessment, you must devise materials for your own individual campaign. This Topic contains a series of activities to enable you to practise designing materials. It is essential that you complete all of these activities so that you will be properly prepared to tackle the controlled assessment.

Designing your materials

This Topic deals with how to design the materials you are going to produce for your practice campaign that you planned in the previous Topic. Now you need to design the materials to promote the aims of your practice campaign.

Having well-designed materials is important in communicating a campaign message. You need to consider what type of materials you are going to produce, such as posters, leaflets, newspaper advertisements etc. Your materials need to be attractive to potential supporters and entice them to find out more. Text and pictures need to be appropriate and appealing, while at the same time reflecting a campaign's purpose.

You need to consider the following points when designing and producing materials for an effective campaign:

- **Structuring your information**
- **Using images and other ways of capturing attention**
- **Using persuasive language**
- **Promoting action**
- **Considering your target audience**
- **Aligning your materials with your campaign**

Structuring your information

Before you start designing your materials, you need to make sure your message has a sensible, logical structure. For example, are the ideas in the right order? Are you repeating yourself unnecessarily? Proofread your text for spelling, punctuation and grammar errors.

ACTIVITY / Media

Layouts   Go to www.criminology.uk.net

Layout The structure of your information includes the way your materials are laid out. This is important whatever materials you are using – whether they are posters, leaflets, T-shirts, coasters etc.

You also need to consider the amount of information you include so as to ensure that your materials are not cluttered. Obviously, the amount of information you include will depend on the type of material you are using. For example, you can't fit as much on a mug as on a leaflet.

ACTIVITY / Structuring your information

Re-visit the websites of the campaigns you compared in Topic 2.1 and 2.2, and look at the materials they have produced.

1. Make notes on the various ways their posters are laid out. For example, the Stop Hate UK campaign has a range of posters on their website.

2. How does the information in the leaflets differ from information in the posters? Are there any similarities between the two?

3. Look at merchandise that the campaigns have produced, such as T-shirts or mugs. How are messages displayed on these?

4. For your own practice campaign, work out some layout designs to fit the materials you are going to produce. For example, if you are going to use a poster, where could you put the main message, an image and contact information for the campaign?

Using images and other ways of capturing attention

It is important that your materials capture people's attention and enable you to get your message across. There are a number of ways you can do this.

Images

Images are the most obvious way of grabbing people's attention and a well-chosen image can make a powerful impact. You need to make sure they communicate your message clearly. Images include items such as photographs, drawings, cartoons, diagrams and symbols. You can use Google Images and other search engines to look for relevant images.

For example, the 'spoon' poster is part of Karma Nirvana's campaign against forced marriage, aimed at young women who are being taken out of the country to be married against their will. It tells them to hide a spoon in their underwear so that it will trigger the alarm at airport security and they can then get help.

Simple images can give important messages.

Some campaigns deal with distressing subjects and images may need to convey this, while not being so shocking that they put off potential supporters. Other campaigns suit more positive images, such as the beneficial effects that could come from the campaign.

Text

Your materials will probably include text. You need to consider the font and sizes you will use. It may be best to use the same font throughout and to vary the size and boldness. A mixture of fonts can look fussy, as well as confusing the reader and detracting from the message.

Don't try to cram too much text into too little space; this will make your message harder to read. Less is more, especially on leaflets and posters.

Colour is important. Text on posters and leaflets should be in darker shades to make it easier to read. Headings, logos or text on merchandise may use reversed text (light colour on a dark background).

Logos Having a logo can be very valuable for a campaign. Using it on all your materials will give your practice campaign a clear identity and give consistency to your message, which will help people recognise its work. Your logo may involve both an image and text. You should also consider the use of colours and fonts as well as the image that you use for your logo.

Radio and TV adverts

You may want to produce a campaign advertisement for radio or TV. If so, you need to write a script for it, with a scenario that would capture and hold the audience's attention. Think

Stop Hate UK's logo. Note how the 'hand' image merges with the text.

about how the language you use would do this (and for TV, think about the images as well). Look out for radio and TV adverts to give you some ideas.

ACTIVITY | **Using images**

Look at the images on the websites of the campaigns you studied in Topics 2.1 and 2.2.

1. Which images draw your attention?
2. What do they tell you about the campaign?
3. Why do you think the campaign selected those particular images?

Using persuasive language

Your language needs to persuade people to get involved and support your practice campaign. Persuasive language uses a range of techniques to get your message across. These include:

- **Repetition** – using a word repeatedly, such as 'carrying a knife can kill, kill, kill'.
- **Triples** – having three ideas to support your case, such as 'dangerous, deadly and disgusting'. This example also uses alliteration, which can be another effective device.
- **Exaggeration** – such as, 'Together we can change anything'.
- **Emotive language** to make your audience feel certain things by using words such as 'evil' or 'deadly', or positive language such as 'love'. For example, Stop Hate UK uses the line 'Spread love, not hate'.
- **Rhetorical questions**, where the answer is implied in the question, such as 'Do you always want to be afraid of this?' (Answer: No.)

- **Speaking directly to the reader** to address them in your campaign, use 'you' and 'we'.
- **Anecdotes and human interest stories** – personal stories that link to the issue.

However, don't go 'over the top' in your efforts to persuade. When you have written your text, re-read it and ask yourself, would you find it credible?

ACTIVITY / Media

Persuasive language   Go to www.criminology.uk.net

Promoting action

Campaigns for change will generally be aiming to engage people in action. Action could range from signing an online petition to attending a demonstration, volunteering to help with the campaign or lobbying a local councillor or Member of Parliament.

You need to make sure that your materials explain what action you want supporters to take and that they encourage them to take this action. For example, if you want people to attend a demonstration, the details of where and when need to be clearly stated on your poster or leaflet. If you want people to sign an online petition, the website where they can access it must be clear and not too complicated.

ACTIVITY / Promoting action

1. Looking back at the campaigns in Topics 2.1 and 2.2, list some of the ways in which their materials encourage action from supporters.
2. For your own practice campaign, how will the design of your materials engage supporters and encourage them to take action?

Considering your target audience

Having a target audience means there are particular people whose attention you want to gain. As we saw in Topic 3.1, part of your campaign planning will have involved identifying your target audience.

Materials that you design must attract your target audience. This means you must have the correct type of materials and the information in them should be engaging to that audience. For example, young people may be more attracted to concise information with a catchy tagline. They may also be more likely than older people to wear a wristband or T-shirt associated with a campaign, especially with an appropriate design.

ACTIVITY / Your target audience

For your own practice campaign:
1. Who is your target audience? Is there more than one group of people?
2. Explain how the design of your materials will gain the attention of your target audience.

Aligning your materials with your campaign

When designing your materials, you need to make sure they are clearly linked to each other. All materials should be giving the same basic message. This could be in the form of a tagline – a short phrase that sums up your campaign and that can be used on any materials you produce.

An example of a tagline is 'Stop hate. Start here' used by Stop Hate UK. If you decide to use a tagline, consider the choice of language carefully and refer to the section on persuasive language above when you are writing it.

ACTIVITY / Media

Your materials

Go to www.criminology.uk.net

Variety in your materials

Although all your materials should carry the same basic message, you can introduce some limited variety. For example, if your aim was to discourage young people from carrying knives, your core message of 'Don't carry a knife' might be at the top of every poster, but underneath you might have 'You can go to jail' on one poster, 'You can shame your parents' on another and so on. This allows you to get across different aspects of your message.

Likewise, if your message is on a T-shirt, you could personalise it so it appears as if the wearer is giving the message, for example 'I support…'

You may want to have different materials for different phases of your practice campaign. For example, if you plan an event, you may have one set of materials to promote the event in advance and then different materials to distribute at the event itself. Although the campaign message is the same, the materials may be different.

For example, posters for an event need to attract visitors to attend, but once people are there you can give them more detailed information about the campaign and opportunities to sign petitions or to become active in the campaign. As well as information leaflets, you could consider balloons for children or wristbands for young people – all with your key message on them.

Using a logo is a good way of keeping an element of consistency throughout all your materials and it also means supporters will always recognise the campaign. (Note the way that a business uses the same logo – like the Nike 'swoosh' for example – on everything it sells, so it achieves instant 'product recognition'.)

T-shirts can carry your message far and wide.

ACTIVITY / Logos and taglines

1. Look back at the campaigns in Topic 2.1 and 2.2. Note their logos and where they appear on any campaign materials. Do they also have a tagline?

2. Design a logo and tagline to use in your campaign. Keep in mind the points in the section above on *Using images and other ways of capturing attention*.

CONTROLLED ASSESSMENT PREPARATION

In the controlled assessment you will need to produce campaign materials. You can practise this by producing materials for the campaign that you planned in Topic 3.1. However, although you can take your notes from this work into the controlled assessment, you will not be allowed to take in previously designed materials.

What you have to do

Using your notes and research from Topic 3.2 *Design materials for use in campaigning for change*, produce well-designed, attractive materials for your campaign for change. Content must be appropriate for changing behaviour. Materials should be visually and verbally stimulating and technically accurate.

Your design should include:

- structuring your information
- using images and other ways of capturing attention
- using persuasive language
- promoting action
- considering your target audience
- aligning your materials with your campaign.

You should consider the design of materials such as:

- leaflets
- advertisements
- posters
- blogs
- social network pages.

How it will be marked

16-20 marks: Well-designed attractive materials are presented. Content is appropriate for changing behaviour. Materials are visually and verbally stimulating and technically accurate.

11-15 marks: Attractive materials are designed with relevant content which stimulates interest. Evidence of persuasive language and clarity of purpose. Some evidence of technical skills.

6-10 marks: Some evidence of materials which are designed with relevant content and which stimulate some interest. Some evidence of persuasive language and clarity of purpose.

1-5 marks: Materials are basic/simple in design. Limited clarity of purpose for the materials.

Justify a campaign for change

Getting started

Working in pairs and taking turns

1. Tell your partner the title of your practice campaign.
2. Explain your reasons for choosing your practice campaign.
3. Explain the ultimate aim of your practice campaign.

The listener should make notes. When you have both outlined your practice campaign to each other, you should each present your partner's campaign to the rest of the class and invite questions.

You should already have planned your practice campaign and designed the materials you are going to use. You now need to justify the choices you have made. This involves three things: presenting your case for action, using evidence to support your case, and your use of persuasive language.

Presenting your case for action

In justifying your practice campaign, you need to present a case explaining clearly why there is a need for it. This will link back to many of the previous Topics in this chapter:

- State clearly the type of under-reported crime you are campaigning about.
- Explain the reasons why the crime you are campaigning about is under-reported (Topic 1.2) and what the consequences of this under-reporting are (Topic 1.3).
- You may want to use relevant statistics to show the extent of the crime. (See Topic 1.6.) You may also want to use examples or case studies to show the impact of the crime.

ACTIVITY / Presenting your case for action

Working on your own and using the information above and your plan from Topic 3.1, write a full justification of the need for action on the topic you have chosen for your practice campaign for change. Aim to write at least a couple of sentences for each of the above bullet points.

Using evidence to support your case

You need to justify the following aspects of your practice campaign:

1. Why you chose its name or tagline.
2. Your methods, including why they would be appropriate and effective in achieving your aim.
3. Your target audience: who they are and why they would respond.
4. Your designs, images, text and layout: what they are and why they would be effective.
5. Finance: explain why your practice campaign would be financially viable.

6. Explain why you feel your timescale is realistic.

7. Any other points you want to make, such as any interesting ideas you took from successful campaigns that you researched.

ACTIVITY / Using evidence to support your case

Working on your own and using points 1 to 7 above, write a full justification of your practice campaign. For each point, you must show the evidence that supports your case.

Your use of persuasive language

Finally, you need to justify your use of persuasive language. You can do this by completing the activity below.

ACTIVITY / Your use of persuasive language

Working on your own and using the list of types of persuasive language in Topic 3.2, identify examples of where you have used this kind of language.

Explain why you feel these examples are likely to be effective in helping you achieve your aims.

CONTROLLED ASSESSMENT PREPARATION

What you have to do

Using your notes and research from Topic 3.3 *Justify a campaign for change*, give a clear, detailed and well-reasoned justification for your practice campaign. Include conclusions that are supported by relevant judgements including:

- presenting your case for action
- using evidence to support your case
- your use of persuasive language.

You should justify your approach and the need for a campaign for change.

How it will be marked

11-15 marks: Clear and detailed justification which is well-reasoned. Conclusions are supported by relevant judgements including the use of persuasive language.

6-10 marks: Some justification is well-reasoned. Response is largely descriptive but includes some appropriate judgements. Persuasive language is used.

1-5 marks: Limited justification of a campaign for change. Evidence is largely descriptive with few judgements.

Preparing for the Unit 1 controlled assessment

When you have completed Unit 1, you will sit the controlled assessment. This section gives you some guidance on how to prepare for it.

What does it involve?

The controlled assessment is in two parts. The tasks cover the eleven Unit 1 Assessment Criteria (ACs) and you must address them all in your answers to the tasks. (They are dealt with in the eleven Topics covered in this book.)

Part One deals with the material you covered in Topics 1.1 to 1.6.

Using the brief In Part One you will be given a brief, which is a scenario describing some crimes. Think of it as a prompt to remind you about some of the ACs that you need to deal with in your answers. You should use the brief wherever the task instructs you to do so.

Part Two In this part, you have to:

● Compare campaigns for change that you studied in Topic 2.1.

● Evaluate the use of different types of media in campaigns that you studied in Topic 2.2.

● Plan, design and justify a campaign linked to an under-reported crime (Topics 3.1, 3.2 and 3.3).

Prepare your file in advance

Before you sit the assessment, it is essential that you have thoroughly prepared your notes for all eleven ACs, because you will need to take them with you into the assessment.

On the next page is a checklist of what you need to do for each AC. Use this to make sure you have written your notes on all of them so that you have everything covered *before* you sit the assessment. For help with making notes for each AC, refer back to the Topic with the same number.

On the day of the assessment

On the day of the controlled assessment, make sure you bring all your Unit 1 materials and have your file in good order.

For Part One you can take in your file, but you can't take in any electronic documents or devices, nor access the internet. Everything you need must be on paper, so if you have any electronic notes you must print them off if you want to take them into the assessment.

For Part Two you are allowed to access the internet but not any electronic files of your own. You are not allowed to take in any previously designed campaign materials for Learning Outcome 3.

AC	What you need to do	Max. mark
Part One (3 hours)		
1.1	Analyse two types of crime evident in the assignment brief. This means you need to identify their characteristics. For each type of crime, include victims, offenders, level of public awareness, whether it is criminal, deviant or both. Give specific examples.	4
1.2	Give a clear and detailed explanation of the reasons for the two unreported crimes in the brief, such as fear, complexity and lack of public concern. Include examples for each reason, e.g. that victims of domestic violence may not report crime due to fear.	4
1.3	Explain the consequences of unreported crime, such as decriminalisation, cultural change and police prioritisation. Include relevant examples such as lack of police prioritisation of under-reported crime such as cannabis use.	4
1.4	Describe media representation of crime, such as newspapers, television and electronic gaming. Give the distinctive features of the representation, such as newspapers focusing on violent crime. Include relevant examples, such as games like Grand Theft Auto.	6
1.5	Explain the impact of a range of media representations on public perception of crimes, such as moral panic, stereotyping of criminals and changing public concerns and attitudes. Include examples such as the moral panic about mods and rockers.	6
1.6	Evaluate crime statistics including Home Office statistics and the Crime Survey for England and Wales. Give an overall assessment of the strengths and limitations of each, with a justification for your assessment. Include reference to reliability, validity, ethics and purpose of each method.	6
Part Two (5 hours)		
2.1	Make a clear and detailed comparison of a range of relevant campaigns for change. Make explicit links to the planned campaign with reference to specific and appropriate sources to support your conclusions.	10
2.2	Make a clear and detailed evaluation of the effectiveness of a range of media used in relevant campaigns for change. Provide clear evidence of well-reasoned judgements to support your conclusions.	15
3.1	Produce a detailed plan of your own campaign, including aims and objectives, justification of why it is needed, your target audience, methods and materials, finances, timescales and resources. Be clear and accurate in all sections and give realistic timings and costings for your campaign.	10
3.2	Present designs for your materials, including screen shots of websites, leaflets and posters, designs of merchandise such as T-shirts, mugs, wristbands etc. You should have a range of materials.	20
3.3	Justify your campaign. Explain why it is necessary. Outline the evidence that supports your case. Explain how the language you have used helps to persuade people to support your campaign.	15
TOTAL		100

CRIMINOLOGICAL THEORIES

Overview

What do we mean by crime and how do we distinguish it from deviance? We begin this Unit by examining these terms, before looking at how crime is socially constructed. Using examples of changes in the law, we examine how and why what counts as 'crime' varies between times, places and cultures. This links to what you learned in Unit 1, Topics 1.5 and 2.1, about how the media and campaigns help to construct our perceptions of criminality and under-reported crimes.

There have been many attempts to understand why people commit crime. For example, are some people 'born criminals' – or is their behaviour the result of their upbringing and social environment? We describe a range of different criminological theories that aim to explain criminality and we use case studies to examine how these theories can be applied to different criminals and types of crime.

How effective are these theories in understanding the causes of criminality? Can they explain all the many kinds of crime, or are they better at explaining one type rather than another? We evaluate the usefulness of the different theories by examining the strengths and limitations of each one.

Policymakers have searched for solutions to the problem of crime and they have developed many different policies aimed at preventing it. We examine a range of these policies and how they have been influenced by criminological theories. We then look at how social changes have influenced policies in relation to issues like racism and LGBT rights. In Unit 1 we examined campaigns to change crime policies and we return to this theme at the end of Unit 2 by looking at campaigns to change policies on crimes such as stalking.

Compare criminal behaviour and deviance

Getting Started

Working with a partner

1. Imagine you are waiting for and then getting on a bus. What rules do you follow?

2. Now discuss how you would feel and what you would do if someone does not follow those rules.

3. Share your feelings with your class.

Norms, values and moral codes

This Topic is about crime and deviance, about their meaning and their similarities and differences. A useful starting point is to say that both crime and deviance challenge or threaten accepted values and norms of behaviour. We therefore need to begin by looking at these two terms.

Norms and values

Values are general principles or guidelines for how we should live our lives. They tell us what is right and wrong, good and bad.

Norms While values lay down general principles or guidelines, norms are specific rules or socially accepted standards that govern people's behaviour in particular situations.

An example of a value that is found in all societies is respect for human life. Other values may be specific to particular societies. For example, societies such as the UK and the USA place a high value on individuals accumulating personal wealth, which is seen as a worthy goal to pursue.

By contrast, many traditional societies, such as those of Native American peoples, place a high value on the duty of individuals to share their wealth with the group. Such societies also generally place a higher value on respect for their elders.

The norms of a given society are linked to its values. For example, cultures that place a high value on respect for elders usually have specific rules (norms) about how elders are to be approached or addressed. It may be forbidden to look directly at them when speaking to them, to interrupt them, or to openly disobey or disagree with them. We can see in this example how one value or general principle (respect for elders) underlies a range of specific rules or norms of behaviour.

ACTIVITY / Research

Norms

Go to www.criminology.uk.net

Moral codes

The term 'moral code' (or 'ethical code' or 'code of ethics') is often used to describe a set of basic rules, values and principles held by an individual, group, organisation or society as a whole.

A moral code or code of ethics may be written down. For example, the Police Code of Ethics is a written guide to the core principles and standards that officers are expected to uphold in their work.

The Police Code lays down nine policing principles: accountability, integrity, openness, fairness, leadership, respect, honesty, objectivity and selflessness. For instance, the principle of fairness requires officers to oppose discrimination and make decisions without prejudice. Some police forces now require officers to sign the Code to show their commitment to its principles.

ACTIVITY / Moral codes

Write your own personal moral code. What are the key principles, beliefs and values you feel you should live by?

Defining deviance

Deviance is any behaviour that differs from normal. In other words, it is behaviour that is unusual, uncommon or out of the ordinary in some way. It could be unusual in one of three different ways:

- **Behaviour that is unusual and *good*,** such as heroically risking one's own life to save someone else.
- **Behaviour that is unusual and *eccentric or bizarre*,** such as talking to the trees in the park, or hoarding huge quantities of old newspapers.
- **Behaviour that is unusual and *bad or disapproved of*,** such as physically attacking someone for no reason.

Although all these definitions of deviance are valid, it is the last one that is most relevant to criminologists. This type of deviance involves doing something forbidden or regarded as unacceptable. In other words, it involves breaking a rule or norm of some kind.

This rule-breaking leads to a critical, hostile or disapproving reaction from others. These 'others' might be society as a whole or a sub-group within society and their reaction may involve punishing the deviant in some way.

ACTIVITY / Media

Defining deviance   Go to www.criminology.uk.net

Forms of deviance Societies have many different rules and therefore deviance, which involves breaking these rules, can take many different forms. These can range from extremely serious acts such as rape, murder or arson to very trivial things such as queue-jumping.

Formal and informal sanctions against deviance

As we saw above, forms of deviance regarded as praiseworthy or odd tend not to lead to punishments. However, deviance that is disapproved of is likely to lead to negative sanctions – that is, punishments of various kinds. Sanctions can be formal or informal:

- **Formal sanctions** are ones imposed by official bodies such as the police, courts, schools and other institutions. They are punishments for breaking formal written rules or laws. For example, courts may fine an offender for theft; schools may exclude pupils for bullying.

- **Informal sanctions** are used where the rules are not formally written down and are perhaps 'unspoken'. When someone breaks these rules, others show their disapproval in informal ways, such as refusing to speak to them, telling them off, a slap on the wrist etc.

> **Question**
>
> What informal sanctions might you use if a friend lets you down in some way?

Positive sanctions Sanctions can also be positive, such as rewards for behaviour that society approves of. Examples include medals for bravery or for sporting achievement and praise from a parent or teacher. Like negative sanctions, they can be formal or informal.

Social control All sanctions, formal or informal, positive or negative, are forms of social control – that is, ways in which society seeks to control our behaviour and ensure that we conform to its norms and behave as others expect us to.

ACTIVITY / Discussion

Sanctions against deviance   Go to www.criminology.uk.net

Defining criminal behaviour

A useful starting point for defining criminal behaviour is to say that it is a form of deviance that involves serious, harmful acts that are a wrong against society. These acts are regarded as so disruptive that the state must intervene on behalf of society to forbid them and to punish them by law. We therefore need to look first at the legal definition of criminal behaviour.

The legal definition of criminal behaviour

In law, criminal behaviour is any action that is forbidden by the criminal law. For a court to consider a defendant's action to be a crime, the action must normally have two elements:

- **actus reus,** which is Latin for 'a guilty act'
- **mens rea,** meaning 'a guilty mind'.

In other words, the defendant must have done something that the law forbids *and* they must have done so with bad intentions. However, there are two important exceptions to this principle:

Strict liability In some cases, mens rea is not required – the wrongful act on its own is enough to convict someone. Many health and safety laws operate on this basis. A factory owner who is negligent and fails to safeguard dangerous machinery is liable for the injuries to workers resulting from this, even if the owner had no intention to harm them.

Most strict liability offences are 'regulatory' offences: they aim at regulating how businesses behave. However, strict liability also applies to other situations, such as speeding or watching TV without a licence. These are offences, even if you didn't intend to do wrong.

Self-defence Assaulting someone (an actus reus) with the deliberate intention to harm them (a mens rea) is usually a criminal act. However, if it is done in self-defence it is not a crime – so long as the force used was reasonable in the situation.

The social definition of criminal behaviour

Although the law does define many harmful acts as crimes, not all harmful acts are in fact criminal. For example, anti-pollution laws often specify how much of a pollutant a firm can legally emit, even though this may still harm the environment. And not all criminal acts are particularly harmful. Many trivial or victimless acts are still classed as crimes.

Rather than relying solely on the legal definition, therefore, we can gain a better understanding of criminal behaviour by considering how it is defined socially. This includes the following aspects.

Differing views

The public often have a different view of what acts are 'really' crimes, as compared with the legal definitions of crimes. For example, the following people may not see themselves as criminals: fare-dodgers; motorists who go a little over the speed limit; users of soft drugs; workers who take home stationery from the office.

Law enforcement

Not all criminal laws are enforced; some come low on the list of priorities for police. For example, white collar crimes are often complex, costly and time-consuming to investigate and prosecute. And police may feel enforcing laws against possession of soft drugs is both unpopular and a waste of time.

Law-making

Not all acts that people think ought to be made into crimes have laws passed against them. Which actions get officially made illegal often depends on who has the power to influence the law-makers, such as the media, campaigning pressure groups or big business.

Sometimes, laws are changed to reflect changes in public opinion, with some actions being decriminalised and other, previously legal ones being redefined as crimes. For example, stalking did not become a specific offence until the Protection of Freedoms Act was passed in 2012.

Is enough done to enforce the law against speeding?

However, there is no straight one-to-one relationship between what the public feel should or shouldn't be a crime, and what the law actually says *is* a crime. An unpopular law may sometimes remain in place, while an action that most people strongly disapprove of may remain legal. We shall deal with changes in the law in more detail in Topic 1.2.

Acts that are criminal

In terms of the legal definition, criminal acts are ones that break the law. However, there are many different kinds of criminal acts, which we can classify in terms of their seriousness or their subject matter.

Seriousness of the offence

In the UK, the law distinguishes between two main types of offence:

- **Summary offences** are less serious offences, such as speeding. They are tried by magistrates.
- **Indictable offences** are more serious offences, such as rape or murder. They are tried in a Crown Court before a judge and jury. The sentences that can be imposed are more severe.

In the past, English law used to make a distinction between misdemeanours (minor crimes) and felonies (serious crimes). This distinction is still used in the USA.

Subject matter of the offence

We can also classify a crime in terms of the nature of the act itself. For example, is it a crime of violence or one of dishonesty? Here are some of the main categories of indictable offences.

- **Violence against the person,** e.g. murder, manslaughter and assault.
- **Sexual offences,** e.g. rape, sex trafficking and grooming.
- **Offences against property,** e.g. burglary, theft and robbery.
- **Fraud and forgery,** e.g. frauds by company directors.
- **Criminal damage,** e.g. arson.
- **Drug offences,** e.g. supplying or possessing heroin.
- **Public order offences,** e.g. riot and violent disorder.

Formal sanctions against criminals

Formal sanctions are the penalties laid down by law that can be imposed on those convicted of a crime. These sanctions vary according to the severity of the crime. Sanctions can be imposed by courts or the police, depending on the offence.

Court sanctions

Custodial sentences

Serious offences can be punished with custodial sentences: imprisonment, or detention in a young offenders' institution. The length of the sentence can vary from a matter of days, up to life imprisonment for murder.

Prisoners serving a life sentence are usually eligible to apply for parole after about 15 years, though courts can impose a longer minimum sentence in more serious cases.

Up until 2012, courts could also impose indeterminate sentences (ones with no specific release date) if the offender is a danger to the public. In these cases, the parole board decides if and when the prisoner is fit to be released.

Community sentences

These are served in the community rather than in jail. They include probation orders, restrictions such as curfews, attendance on anger management courses, mandatory drug testing and treatment orders and Community Payback (doing unpaid work in the community, e.g. cleaning off graffiti).

Fines are financial penalties. The size of the fine depends on the seriousness of the offence, whether it is a repeat offence and the offender's ability to pay. Offenders may be allowed to pay in instalments.

Statue representing justice. She wears a blindfold and holds a sword and scales. What do these stand for?

Discharge A *conditional discharge* involves the offender committing no further offence for a given period. If they commit an offence during this period, the court can impose a sentence for the original offence as well as for the new one.

The court may grant an unconditional or *absolute discharge* where the defendant is technically guilty but where punishment would be inappropriate. It is not classed as a conviction.

Police sanctions

In the case of some minor offences, the police can sanction offenders without going to court, by issuing cautions or penalty notices.

Cautions are warnings that can be given by the police or Crown Prosecution Service to anyone aged 10 or over for minor crimes such as graffiti. They are intended for low-level, first-time offending. You must admit to the offence and agree to be cautioned.

You can be arrested and charged if you don't accept the caution. Although a caution is not a criminal conviction, it can be used as evidence of bad character if you go to court for another crime.

Conditional cautions mean you have to stick to certain rules and restrictions, such as going for treatment for drug abuse. If you break the conditions, you could be charged with a crime.

Penalty notices for disorder can be issued for minor crimes such as shoplifting or possession of cannabis. You won't get a conviction if you pay the penalty. If you disagree with the penalty notice, you can go to trial instead.

Other implications of committing a criminal act

As well as the punishment imposed by the court, the offender will also receive a criminal record. Depending on the offence and the court's sentence, there may also be other implications.

- Exclusion from certain occupations, e.g. working with young people.
- They may be placed on the Violent and Sex Offenders Register (ViSOR).
- They may be banned from travelling to certain countries or require special visas.
- There may be restrictions on adoption, jury service and standing for elected office. They may have to declare unspent convictions when obtaining insurance.

ACTIVITY Media

Sentencing

Go to www.criminology.uk.net

Acts that are both criminal and deviant

Most acts that get classified as crimes would be regarded as deviant, that is, as forbidden or unacceptable. Acts such as murder are more or less universally regarded as appalling and intolerable. This is of course one reason why society classifies these forms of deviance as crimes in the first place – to express our extreme disapproval and to back this up with official and severe punishment.

Criminal but not deviant?

However, not all acts that are classified as crimes are particularly serious, and some of them may be widely regarded as not even particularly deviant. For example, while possessing cannabis is a crime, some do not regard it as bad behaviour.

To complicate matters further, society is often divided on whether a particular crime is actually deviant. For example, many other people do see possession of cannabis as morally wrong and hence deviant.

Deviant but not criminal?

The other side of the coin is that acts that some people see as deviant are not always crimes. For example, although homosexual acts between consenting adults are no longer illegal in the UK, some people regard it as morally wrong and hence deviant.

This kind of issue often arises when social attitudes are changing. Attitudes may begin to change towards behaviour that was once both illegal and seen as deviant by almost everyone. Some people may now see it as acceptable and this may lead to a change in the law. However, at the same time, others may continue to see the behaviour as deviant, even though the law has changed. Examples include attitudes towards homosexuality and abortion.

NOW TEST YOURSELF

Practice Question

Compare criminality and deviance with reference to relevant examples. (6 marks)

Source: WJEC Criminology Unit 2 examination 2017

Advice

This question involves looking at both the differences *and* the similarities between criminality and deviance. Start by defining deviance as violating social norms or expected behaviour, and give a couple of examples. At least one of your examples should be of deviance that is regarded as harmful, but it's alright to include an example of harmless deviance (e.g. odd behaviour such as living with 50 cats) or beneficial deviance (e.g. risking one's life to save a stranger) as well.

Next define criminality as a breach of the formal criminal law. Then give a couple of examples of crimes. You can also refer to the kinds of formal and informal sanctions that your examples of crime and deviance might face.

You can note that some behaviour is both criminal and deviant – there can be an overlap between the two – whereas other behaviour may be criminal but not widely seen as deviant (possession of cannabis, perhaps), or deviant but not criminal (such as queue-jumping). Also note that whether or not a particular action is seen as deviant, criminal or both can change over time.

Explain the social construction of criminality

Getting Started

Working with a partner

1. Make a list of examples of:

   a Activities that are illegal in the UK but legal in other countries

   b Activities that are legal in the UK but illegal in other countries

   c Activities that used to be illegal that are now legal in the UK

   d Activities that used to be legal in the UK but are now illegal.

   Can you give any reasons for the differences?

2. Can you think of situations where the same act may be seen as either legal *or* illegal?

3. Share your ideas with the class. What conclusions can you draw about how or why actions are defined as illegal?

What is the social construction of criminality?

The term 'social construction' refers to something that has been made or defined ('constructed') by society, rather than simply occurring naturally. Therefore, what counts as criminality is simply whichever acts a society *defines* as criminal. And of course, one society or culture can define a particular act as criminal and pass a law against it, while another culture sees nothing wrong in it. Likewise, as a society changes over time, its ideas about what is a crime can also change.

ACTIVITY / Media

Social construction   Go to www.criminology.uk.net

In the next two sections, we shall look at some examples of how laws change and vary from culture to culture, and how laws within a society can change over time. All these examples illustrate the key idea that criminality is a social construction.

How laws change from culture to culture

There are many examples of how laws – and therefore what counts as a crime – change or vary from one culture to another.

Polygamy

Polygamy is the practice of having more than one wife or one husband at the same time. There are two forms of polygamy:

- **polygyny**, where a man may take two or more wives
- **polyandry**, where a woman may take two or more husbands.

Where is it legal? Polygyny is legal in 58 countries, while polyandry is confined to a handful of societies, mainly in the Himalayas. Most societies where polygamy is legal are Muslim-majority countries. In five multi-cultural societies with a large Muslim population (India, Malaysia, the Philippines, Singapore and Sri Lanka), the law permits polygamous marriages, but for Muslims only.

Where is it a crime? Polygamy is against the law in most countries. Even many Muslim countries place restrictions on it and in two – Turkey and Tunisia – polygamy is a crime. In the UK, anyone who goes through a marriage ceremony while they are still married to someone else, is committing the crime of bigamy. Bigamy is punishable by up to seven years' imprisonment, a fine or both.

Reasons why the law varies between cultures

- **Religion** The Qur'an permits Muslim men to take up to four wives and this is reflected in the laws of most Muslim-majority countries. In the USA, the Mormon Church practised polygamy until 1890, and it continues to be practised illegally by some fundamentalist Mormon splinter groups.

- **Tradition** Polygamy has traditionally been practised in some African societies, though it has declined sharply in recent decades.

Polygamist Alex Joseph and his wives at home on the Nevada-Utah border, USA.

Adultery

Adultery involves a sexual act between two people, one or both of whom is married to another person. However, what counts as a 'sexual act' may vary between cultures or states.

Where is it a crime? Most societies that criminalise adultery are Muslim-majority countries, though several Christian-majority countries in Africa make adultery a criminal offence, as do the Philippines, Taiwan and 21 U.S. states. Punishment varies widely, from stoning to death (though this is rare), to caning (e.g. in Malaysia and Indonesia), to a fine (in Rhode Island, USA).

Where is it legal? In most countries, including the UK, adultery is not against the law. In India it ceased to be a crime in 2018.

Reasons why the law varies between cultures

- **Religion** Most religions condemn adultery. Not committing adultery is one of the Ten Commandments shared by Christianity, Islam and Judaism. In societies where law-making has been strongly influenced by religion, adultery has often been made a crime.

- **The position of women** Laws against adultery are often found in societies where women occupy a very subordinate position. Usually in such societies, the adultery laws are themselves unequal.

ACTIVITY / Research

Adultery   Go to www.criminology.uk.net

Homosexuality

Sexual acts between members of the same sex are treated as crimes in a number of countries.

Where is it a crime? Male homosexuality is illegal in 72 countries and in 45 so are lesbian relationships. In six countries, conviction can result in the death penalty. In some countries, such as Russia, homosexuality is not illegal but the law bans its 'promotion'. Many countries which do not criminalise homosexuality, nevertheless do not allow same-sex couples to marry or adopt.

Where is it legal? Homosexuality is legal in the UK, Europe and North and South America. Although it is a crime in many Muslim countries, in Indonesia, the world's largest Muslim state by population, it is legal.

Reasons why the law varies between cultures

- **Religion** Many religions, including Christianity, Islam and Judaism, have traditionally condemned homosexuality. Countries where religion has a strong influence over law-making are more likely to have laws making homosexuality a crime. By contrast, in secular societies (ones where religion has less influence), social norms are generally more tolerant of sexual diversity.

- **Public opinion** Polls by the Pew Research Center show higher levels of support for bans on homosexuality in some countries. Some of these are countries where religion has a strong influence (for example, 95% in Egypt believed homosexuality should be rejected) but others, such as Russia, are not.

- **Sexism** The fact that male homosexuality is a crime in more countries than lesbianism is, may be due to sexist assumptions by male lawmakers that women were incapable of same-sex attraction.

Cannabis

Laws on cannabis vary widely between different societies. In general, possession of cannabis for personal use is treated more leniently than growing, importing or supplying (dealing) cannabis.

Where is it a crime? In the UK, possession can be punished with up to 5 years imprisonment and supply with 14 years. However, sentences are typically far lighter and for possession may often be a fine or a discharge. Many other European countries have similar laws relating to cannabis.

Where is it legal? Some places have legalised possession for personal recreational or medical use. Others have also legalised its sale, including Canada and Uruguay. As we saw in Unit 1, Topic 1.3, some countries, such as Portugal, have decriminalised possession for personal use. This means it has been reclassified as a misdemeanour, or minor offence. The offender receives a warning rather than a more severe penalty.

Reasons why the law varies between cultures

- **Different norms and values** Differences in laws on cannabis to some extent reflect differences in norms, values and attitudes between societies. Societies with a greater emphasis on individual freedoms may see drug use as victimless or as an individual's right to do as they wish with their body.

- **Different ideas about how best to control drug use** Lawmakers in some societies take the view that the best way to prevent drugs causing harm is by taking a tough stance to deter their use. They favour severe criminal penalties even for possession of cannabis, which they see as a 'gateway' drug that can lead to addiction to hard drugs such as heroin.

  By contrast, lawmakers in other societies see legalisation or decriminalisation as a way to take cannabis out of the hands of criminal suppliers and to reduce the harm by enabling users to get help for their problems.

Question

Can you think of any other arguments for or against legalising the possession of cannabis for personal use?

How laws change over time

Just as laws may change from one culture to another, so they often change over time within a given society. For instance, in Unit 1, Topic 1.5, we saw how moral panics about illegal raves and dangerous dogs led to changes in the law. In this section, we look at some further examples of changes in laws that have occurred over time.

Homosexuality

Laws on same-sex relationships have changed greatly in the UK in the recent decades.

Changes over time

In the UK, all homosexual acts between men were made a crime in 1885, with a maximum sentence of life imprisonment. However, homosexual acts between males aged 21 or over were legalised in England and Wales in 1967, in Scotland in 1980 and Northern Ireland in 1982 (lesbian acts had never been illegal).The age of consent was reduced to 18 in 1994 and then equalised with heterosexuals at 16 in 2000.

The British introduced many laws into their colonies during the period of the British Empire. For example, in 1861, they introduced a law in India making homosexuality a crime. This law was struck down by India's Supreme Court in 2018 and homosexuality is no longer an offence.

Reasons why the law changed

The Wolfenden Report After the Second World War, there was an increase in prosecutions of gay men and by 1954 over 1,000 were in prison. Following several trials of well-known figures, the government set up a committee under Sir John Wolfenden to consider reform of the law.

After gathering evidence from police, psychiatrists, religious leaders and gay men (whose identity had to be concealed), the committee's report published in 1957 recommended that homosexual acts in private between consenting adults over 21 be legalised.

Campaigns The Homosexual Law Reform Society, made up of leading public figures, successfully campaigned for the change in the law that legalised gay sex in 1967. Further campaigns by Stonewall and the Campaign for Homosexual Equality led eventually to equalising the age of consent at 16.

Politicians such as Roy Jenkins supported the campaign for change and as Home Secretary he introduced the necessary legislation in 1967. Others since have introduced further legislation such as the 2010 Equality Act which outlaws discrimination of grounds of sexual orientation.

Human rights In India the main reason for the change in the law was the decision of the Supreme Court that the state has no right to control citizens' private lives. In the UK this concern with equal rights also underlies changes in the law on homosexuality.

Gay Pride demonstration. Stonewall has been campaigning for LGBT equal rights since 1989.

Drug laws

Drug laws have changed over time in many countries. In some cases, possession of certain drugs has been made a criminal offence, while in other cases it has been decriminalised, as in the case of Portugal below.

Changes over time

The Portuguese case is an interesting example. From 2001, possession of drugs was changed from a crime to a civil offence, if the quantity involved was less than for a ten-day personal supply. The new law applied to both 'hard' drugs such as heroin and 'soft' ones such as cannabis.

The background to the change in the law is interesting. From the 1930s until 1975 Portugal had been ruled by a right-wing dictatorship as a 'closed' and strictly regulated society (Coca Cola was banned and citizens even had to obtain a licence to own a cigarette lighter!).

After a revolution in 1975, Portugal became a democracy and the increased openness of the country led to a large influx of drugs. Very soon, Portugal had the highest rates of heroin addiction in Europe, as well as soaring rates of HIV infection caused by needle-sharing among addicts.

Public health The thinking behind decriminalisation was that drug use should be regarded as a public health issue aimed at harm reduction, rather than an issue for the criminal justice system. Users are referred to health and other support services rather than being prosecuted.

Since the change in the law, drug use has fallen sharply. HIV infections among addicts are almost non-existent and deaths from drugs are now the lowest in Europe: around 4 per million of the population, compared with figures for England and Wales of around 44 per million.

Reasons why the law changed

The basic reason for the change was the sudden and rapid growth in the scale of drug addiction in Portugal after 1975: by the 1990s, one in every 100 of the population was addicted to heroin. This led to calls for drastic action to tackle the problem.

It was also felt that, as a relatively poor country, the new law would reduce the costs resulting from drug use and one source points to a saving of 18%.

ACTIVITY Media

Legalising drugs

Go to www.criminology.uk.net

Gun control laws

Changes over time In the UK, laws governing access to firearms changed following two mass shootings:

- In 1987, Michael Ryan, an unemployed antique dealer, shot and killed 16 people in Hungerford, Berkshire.
- In 1996, 16 children and one teacher were shot dead at Dunblane primary school near Stirling in Scotland by Thomas Hamilton, an unemployed former scout leader.

Most of the weapons used, including several semi-automatics capable of rapidly firing multiple rounds, were legally held.

As a result, the law was tightened in 1997 following a government enquiry led by a senior former judge, Lord Cullen. John Major's Conservative government introduced an act banning all handguns except .22 single shot weapons. Following Labour's victory in the general election later that year, Tony Blair's government introduced a second Firearms (Amendment) Act, banning the remaining handguns as well. Apart from some historic and sporting weapons, it is now illegal to own a handgun in Great Britain.

Reasons why the law changed

The main reason for the change in the law was the public outcry following Hungerford and especially Dunblane. However, two important campaigns helped to press for a change in the law:

- **The Gun Control Network**, set up by lawyers, academics and parents of victims to campaign for tighter gun control laws.
- **The Snowdrop Campaign**, started by bereaved Dunblane parents and their friends, organised a petition and collected 750,000 signatures calling for a change in the law.

ACTIVITY	Media

Gun control   Go to www.criminology.uk.net

Laws relating to children

Childhood is a very good example of social construction. Although everyone goes through a biological stage of physical immaturity in the first years of life, how society has defined this phase has varied greatly over time.

In British society today, the dominant idea of childhood is of a special time of happiness – 'the best years of your life' (though this is not to say that reality always lives up to this ideal). We see children as fundamentally different from adults: vulnerable, innocent and in need of protection and nurturing. As a result, in many ways children are kept separate from the adult world and its dangers.

Changes over time However, it has not always been like this. The historian Philippe Ariès argues that until the 13th century, 'the idea of childhood did not exist'. Children were put out to work from an early age and were in effect 'mini-adults' with the same rights and duties as everyone else. The law often made no distinction between children and adults, and children could face the same severe punishments as those handed out to adults.

Brick factory, present day Peru. Child labour was widespread in Britain until the late 19th century.

Over time, the idea of childhood as a separate stage in life gradually developed and society became more 'child-centred'. Parents invest a great deal in their children both emotionally and financially, and the state takes a great interest in their wellbeing.

Changes in the law

As a result of growing concern for children and their welfare, there have been important changes in the laws relating to children in the last two centuries. These changes reflect how society's view of childhood has changed over time.

- **Laws excluding children from paid work**. In the 19th century, children as young as six were widely used in cotton mills, coalmines and other industries. A series of Factory Acts gradually excluded children from the workplace.
- **Compulsory schooling** introduced in 1880 ensured a basic education for all and also had the effect of keeping children out of paid work.
- **Child protection and welfare legislation,** such as the 2004 Children Act made the child's welfare the fundamental principle underpinning the work of agencies such as social services.
- **Children's rights** The Children Act defines parents as having 'responsibilities' rather than 'rights' in relation to children, while the United Nations Convention on the Rights of the Child (1989) lays down basic rights such as entitlement to healthcare and education, protection from abuse and the right to participate in decisions that affect them, such as custody cases.
- **Laws and policies that only apply to children**, such as minimum ages for a wide range of activities, from sex to smoking, reinforce the idea that children are different from adults and so different rules must be applied to their behaviour.

Question

Should children have all the same rights as adults? If so, from what age?

ACTIVITY / Research

Legal age limits

Go to www.criminology.uk.net

Laws concerning physical punishment

In the past, physical punishment for criminal behaviour was common. At various times in British history, criminals (depending on their crime) could be punished by:

- **capital punishment** (execution) by hanging, not only for murder but also for less serious crimes. For example, the 1723 Black Act made over 50 offences of theft and poaching into capital crimes.
- **corporal punishment** has included flogging, birching (caning), branding with hot irons and being put in the stocks.

Changes in the law

Over time, the number of offences carrying the death penalty was reduced, until it remained only for murder and treason. Capital punishment was finally abolished in Britain in 1965. Corporal punishment has also gradually disappeared. For example, flogging in the armed forces was abolished in 1881 and all corporal punishment of offenders was abolished in 1967.

Reasons for the changes

- Capital punishment is now regarded as a breach of the most basic human right – the right to life.

- Nothing can be done to correct a miscarriage of justice, where a person executed is later proven to have been innocent.
- The death penalty does not appear to act as a deterrent. Most murders are committed in the heat of the moment without thought to the possible punishment.
- Some writers argue that changes in the law are the result of a long-term decline in violence. Norbert Elias argues that society has undergone a 'civilising process' over the last 500 years. Physical punishment to control behaviour has gradually been replaced by self-control. Society has moved away from the idea of physical violence, as shown by the disappearance of spectacles like bear-baiting or public executions.

Bentley was hanged for murder in 1953. His conviction was quashed in 1998.

How laws are applied differently according to circumstances in which actions occur

In theory, the law is applied equally to everyone: two different people suspected of the same crime should be treated in the same way by the justice system. However, this is not always the case. There are several ways in which the laws may be applied differently according to the circumstances in which a criminal act occurs.

Differential enforcement of the law

The law is not always enforced equally. For example, as we saw in Unit 1, Topic 1.5, moral panics about certain crimes and the situations in which they occur can lead to offenders being treated more harshly by the courts.

Moral panics Those convicted of relatively minor offences committed during the London riots of 2011, such as theft, were more likely to receive custodial sentences than similar cases committed under 'normal' conditions. Likewise, the courts imposed more severe sentences on youths convicted of offences during the moral panic over mods and rockers in the 1960s. In these cases, the stiffer sentences were often handed down to 'teach young people a lesson' and to deter others.

Typifications Another way in which the law may be enforced differently against similar cases is shown by the work of Chambliss. Chambliss studied two groups of youths, the middle-class

'Saints' and the working-class 'Roughnecks'. He found that, while both groups committed offences, the police enforced the law more strictly against the Roughnecks.

Chambliss's research supports that of Cicourel. As we saw in Unit 1, Topic 1.5, Cicourel argues that police officers hold typifications – ideas about what a 'typical criminal' is like. For example, they are more likely to regard working-class rather than middle-class individuals with suspicion, resulting in more arrests for this group.

Similarly, Piliavin and Briar found that 'situational factors' play a large part in police officers' decisions to stop or arrest a person. These include the individual's class, ethnicity, age, attitude towards the officer, and place and time of day or night. Thus two different individuals can commit the same offence but one may be more likely than the other to be arrested.

Age of criminal responsibility

Two people may commit the same criminal act but will be treated differently by the law if one of them is below the age of criminal responsibility. This is the age below which a child is deemed not to have the capacity to commit a crime. The logic behind this is that children below a certain age are unable to understand the full meaning of the act they have committed and so cannot be held responsible for it in the same way.

The age of criminal responsibility varies from place to place. In England, Wales and Northern Ireland it is 10 years. No other country in Europe has a lower age of criminal responsibility than this. In Scotland the age of criminal responsibility is 12.

Questions

1. From what age should children be held responsible for crimes they commit?

2. At what age should young people face the same punishments as adults?

Youth courts and punishments Children or young people who commit a crime may be treated differently by the justice system. Most countries have separate courts to deal with offenders below a certain age.

In England and Wales, youth courts are special magistrates' courts that hear cases involving people aged 10 to 17. Youth courts are less formal: defendants are called by their first name, and members of the public are not normally allowed in. The court cannot send anyone to prison but can impose sentences including a detention and training order carried out in a secure centre.

Homicide

There are three special defences contained in the Homicide Act 1957 which exist solely for the offence of murder, where the defendant can plead not guilty despite having killed someone:

- **Diminished responsibility** If a defendant can show that their mental condition substantially reduced their ability to understand what they were doing or form a rational judgment, this reduces the conviction to manslaughter.

- **Loss of control** is a partial defence that may reduce the offence to manslaughter.

- **Automatism** A crime must be a voluntary act – the defendant must have consciously chosen to commit it. If they can show that it was involuntary, they can plead the defence of automatism.

ACTIVITY / Research

You be the judge   Go to www.criminology.uk.net

NOW TEST YOURSELF

Practice Question

With reference to examples, analyse how laws change due to time, place and culture. (9 marks)

Source: WJEC Criminology Unit 2 examination 2017

Answer by Chloe

Laws exist to tackle crime, and crime is socially constructed, so an action that is a crime at one time, place or culture can be legal at another. Homosexuality is now legal in Britain but was illegal before the 1967 Sexual Offences Act. One reason for this is that attitudes and values have changed. We now believe in human rights – the state has no right to interfere in personal relationships. Another reason is secularisation (decline of religion). Churches opposed homosexuality, but religion has less influence today. The law has also changed due to campaigners like Stonewall, the influence on public opinion of the Wolfenden Report, and support from politicians. A further legal change is the Marriage (Same Sex Couples) Act 2013 allowing same-sex couples to wed.

> Good link to social construction. Relevant example and explains both why and how the law changed.

Meanwhile, homosexuality remains illegal in many places, especially those with a strongly religious culture: over 70 countries outlaw male homosexuality and in six countries it can lead to a death sentence.

> Good contrast to show how laws vary between places and cultures.

UK gun control laws have also changed over time, due to the impact of the Dunblane and Hungerford massacres, where gunmen killed 33 people, using legally held weapons. Public outrage, campaigning by the Gun Control Network and the Snowdrop petition's 750,000 signatures pressured government to ban all handgun ownership in 1997. What had been acceptable to British culture became unacceptable and illegal. By contrast, in the USA the constitution guarantees the right to bear arms and gun ownership is so widespread it can be seen as a cultural norm for many Americans.

> Good, detailed example. Shows how and why the law changed: public outrage, campaigning and cultural change.

Drug laws vary over time and place. In Portugal there was a huge rise in addiction after the 1970s, causing a public health crisis. To tackle it, possession was decriminalised and users were given access to health care instead of prosecution, resulting in a big drop in usage, HIV infections and drug deaths – now 11 times lower than England, where possession remains a crime. Changed attitudes by the authorities and the need to deal with the health impact (including soaring treatment costs) were the main reasons for the change.

> Well explained, detailed example, showing reasons for and results of change in the law.

Finally, acts which were legal can become illegal due to changes in cultural values or campaigns. In Britain, these include child labour, capital and corporal punishment, and stalking.

> Nice way to finish, by showing legal acts can become illegal over time.

Overall comments

This is a Band Three (top band) response. Chloe uses several detailed examples of changes in laws due to time, place and culture. Through her examples, she explains how the changes occurred, for example through campaigning, public pressure and the attitudes of the authorities. She deals with reasons why they occurred, including changing attitudes and values, human rights, the health crisis caused by drugs and public outrage over gun deaths. She uses contrasts between different countries in relation to the examples of homosexuality, gun control and drugs to bring out variations in the laws between different places and cultures.

Describe biological theories of criminality

Getting Started

Working with a partner, answer the following questions.

1. What does it mean to say that some people are 'born criminals'?
2. Crime often runs in families. Why do you think this is?
3. Why does drinking alcohol sometimes lead to criminal behaviour? What kinds of crimes do you associate with alcohol?

Criminologists have developed many theories about the causes of crime, but we can group them into three main types: biological, individualistic and sociological theories. In this Topic we shall describe biological theories of criminality. In the next two Topics we shall describe individualistic and sociological theories.

Biological theories of criminality

The basic idea behind all biological theories of criminality is that criminals are biologically different from non-criminals and this difference causes them to commit crime. We shall look at four types of biological explanation for criminality:

1. **Physiological theories** focusing on criminals' physical characteristics
2. **Genetic theories** that see criminality as inherited
3. **Brain injuries and disorders** that cause people to offend
4. **Biochemical explanations** involving factors such as hormones in offending.

Physiological theories

These biological theories claim that the physical features of criminals differ from those of non-criminals.

Lombroso's theory: 'born criminals'

The first physiological theory of criminality was put forward by the Italian doctor Cesare Lombroso in 1876. He argued that criminals were physically different from non-criminals and he spent many years measuring and recording details of the heads and faces of thousands of prisoners.

From this research Lombroso concluded that criminals could be identified by their distinctive physical features, such as enormous jaws, high cheek bones, handle-shaped ears, prominent eyebrow arches, exceptionally long arms, large eye sockets and extremely acute eyesight. He claimed that different types of criminal had different facial features. For example, murderers had 'aquiline' noses like the beak of an eagle, whereas thieves had flattened noses.

Atavism

Lombroso saw criminals as atavistic, that is, as throwbacks to an earlier, primitive stage of evolution. They were pre-social, unable to control their impulses and had a reduced sensitivity to pain (which in his view was why they often had tattoos). Thus, he argued that criminals were like 'savages' or even apes (hence the long arms!). In a more 'primitive' society, he claimed, they would be normal, but in modern society they are abnormal.

Ex-contract killer 'Popeye' Velásquez served 23 years for killing over 250 people for the Colombian mafia.

In Lombroso's view, such people were 'born criminals' that we could identify scientifically by 'reading' their bodies for the physical characteristics that marked them out as different. Lombroso's is very much an 'us and them' theory. We are normal and they, the criminals, are abnormal and fundamentally different from us.

Lombroso went on to identify two other types of criminal that he saw as biologically different: 'insane criminals' and 'epileptic criminals'.

Sheldon's somatotypes theory

William Sheldon also saw criminals as physically different from non-criminals. In his view, certain body types or 'somatotypes' are linked to criminal behaviour. He identifies three somatotypes:

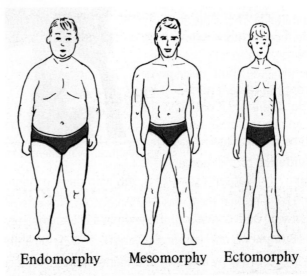

Sheldon's somatotypes. Can body type predict criminality?

- **Endomorphs** are rounded, soft and tending to fat, lacking muscle or tone, with wide hips. Their personality is sociable, relaxed, comfortable and outgoing.

- **Ectomorphs** are thin and fragile, lacking both fat and muscle. They are flat chested, with narrow hips and shoulders, a thin face and high forehead. Their personality is self-conscious, fragile, inward looking, emotionally restrained and thoughtful.

- **Mesomorphs** are muscular and hard bodied, with very little fat and strong limbs, broad shoulders and a narrow waist. Their personality is adventurous, sensation-seeking, assertive and domineering, and they enjoy physical activity.

Sheldon argued that mesomorphs are the somatotype most likely to engage in crime. They are more likely to be attracted by the risk-taking it involves and their imposing physique and assertiveness can be important assets in crime.

Genetic theories

If crime is inborn, as Lombroso claimed, then presumably it is passed down from parent to child. If so, this might explain why crime often runs in families. For example, the Cambridge Study in Delinquent Development, a longitudinal study that has been running since 1961, found that out of 397 families, half of all criminal convictions came in just 23 families. Similarly, Osborn and West found that sons of criminal fathers were much more likely to have a criminal record too.

Twin studies

Why does crime often run in families? Genetic theories explain it as follows. Family members who are blood relatives (e.g. parents and their children; siblings) share many of the same genes. Therefore if one member has 'criminal genes', it is likely that his or her blood relatives will have them too, and this is why criminals have relatives who are also criminals.

Genetic theories have used studies of identical twins as a way to test their theory of criminality. This is because identical or monozygotic (MZ) twins share exactly the same genes – they both developed from the same fertilised egg. Therefore if one twin is criminal, the other twin ought to be criminal too.

Identical twins, identical genes. Does this mean identical risk of criminality?

Evidence for this comes from Christiansen's study of 3,586 twin pairs in Denmark.

- He found that there was a 52% concordance rate between MZ twins; that is, where one identical twin had a conviction, there was a 52% chance of the other twin also having a conviction.
- But among non-identical (dyzgotic or DZ) twins, there was only a 22% chance.

A similar study by Ishikawa and Raine found a 44% concordance rate for identical twins but only 21.6% for non-identical twins.

Adoption studies

Researchers have also used adoption studies to test for a genetic cause of crime. These studies compare adopted children both to their biological birth parents and to their adopted parents.

The thinking behind adoption studies is that an adopted child (especially if adopted soon after birth) shares the same *environment* as their adoptive parents, but the same *genes* as their biological parents. If we find that the adoptee's behaviour in regard to criminality is more similar to their *birth* parents' behaviour, this would support a genetic explanation.

Question

Why might it be important to know whether or not the adoption took place soon after birth?

Evidence Mednick et al examined data on over 14,000 adopted sons in Denmark from 1924 to 1947. They found that sons were more likely to have a criminal record if a *birth* parent also had a record (a concordance rate of 20%). This supports a *genetic* explanation. By contrast, they found that a smaller proportion (14.7%) had a criminal record if their *adoptive* parent had one.

Hutchings and Mednick compared adoptees with and without criminal records. They found that adoptees with criminal records were more likely to have biological parents with criminal records than adoptees whose birth parents did not have criminal records.

ACTIVITY Media

Twin and adoption studies   Go to www.criminology.uk.net

Jacob's XYY study

Abnormality of the sex chromosomes is another possible genetic cause of criminality. Chromosomes are made of DNA and protein, and they are found in the nucleus of our cells. Each chromosome contains many genes. Chromosomes carry all the genetic information that we inherit from our parents.

We normally have 46 chromosomes, arranged in 23 pairs. We inherit half of each pair from each parent. One pair consists of our sex chromosomes and determines whether we are male or female. Our mother's two female chromosomes are known as XX and our father's two male chromosomes are XY.

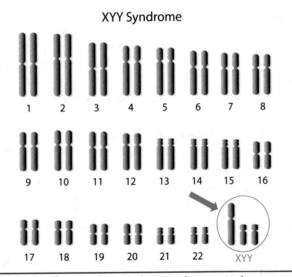

The 'super male syndrome', showing the extra Y chromosome.

Because we inherit one chromosome from each parent, we will have either:

● two Xs: one from each parent. If we have XX we will be female.

● or an X from our mother and a Y from our father. If we have XY, we will be male. It's the Y chromosome that makes a child male.

However, sometimes there are abnormalities. One abnormality is an extra Y (male) chromosome. This is known as XYY syndrome and has been labelled 'super male syndrome'. Men with XYY syndrome tend to be very tall and well built, and of low intelligence. Jacob et al claim that men with XYY syndrome are more aggressive and potentially violent than other males.

Evidence This claim is based on studies of imprisoned criminals, such as those in secure psychiatric hospitals, where a higher than average proportion of the inmates were found to have XYY syndrome. Many had histories of aggression and violent assault. Price and Whatmore found XYY males to be immature and unstable, with a strong tendency to commit seemingly motiveless property crimes.

Question

What problems might there be in drawing conclusions about the causes of criminality from only studying inmates of secure psychiatric hospitals?

Brain injuries and disorders

Certain diseases, injuries and malfunctions of the brain have been linked to criminal behaviour.

Brain injuries

There are some rare cases of brain injuries being identified as the cause of criminality, such as the case of the railway worker Phineas Gage, whose personality changed after a major brain injury. Some studies have shown that prisoners are more likely than non-prisoners to have suffered brain injuries.

ACTIVITY / Media

Brain injury   Go to www.criminology.uk.net

Diseases

Some brain diseases have been linked with criminal or anti-social behaviour. For example, in the 1920s, epidemics of *encephalitis lethargica* among children were linked to destructiveness, impulsiveness, arson and abnormal sexual behaviour. Other brain diseases, including senile dementia, Huntington's disease and brain tumours have also been linked to various forms of deviant or anti-social behaviour.

Abnormal brainwave activity Brainwave activity is measured by an electroencephalograph (EEG). Some studies show abnormal EEG readings among 'clearly insane' murderers and psychopathic criminals.

Biochemical explanations

Biochemical substances and processes have been suggested as possible causes of criminal behaviour, because of their effect on brain chemistry and mental processes. These include sex hormones, blood sugar levels and substance abuse.

Sex hormones

Males Overproduction or underproduction of hormones may cause emotional disturbances that lead to criminal behaviour. Males of most species are more aggressive than females, and the male sex hormone testosterone has been linked with crimes such as murder and rape. Similarly, Ellis and Coontz point out that testosterone levels peak from puberty to the early 20s and this age range correlates with the highest crime rates in males.

ACTIVITY / Media

Testosterone   Go to www.criminology.uk.net

Females Pre-menstrual tension (PMT), post-natal depression and lactation (breastfeeding) have all been accepted as partial defences for women charged with crimes ranging from shoplifting to infanticide, on the grounds that the hormones involved have affected the defendant's judgment, mood or self-control.

Blood sugar levels

Hypoglycaemia (low blood sugar) can trigger aggressive reactions. Studies show a link between low blood sugar and alcohol abuse. Drinking large quantities of alcohol can induce hypoglycaemia and increase aggression. Alcohol consumption is closely linked to crimes of violence.

Schoenthaler claims that by lowering the daily sucrose intake of young offenders, he could reduce the level of their anti-social behaviour.

Substance abuse

This involves the intake of drugs and other substances. Some are legal (e.g. alcohol and glues) or medically prescribed (e.g. barbiturates), while others are illegal (e.g. cannabis, MDMA, LSD, heroin and cocaine).

Saunders calculated that alcohol played a significant role in about 1,000 arrests per day. In the USA, Flanzer estimated that 80% of family violence cases involved alcohol. Cocaine and 'crack' are also closely linked with violence, whereas cannabis, heroin and MDMA tend to reduce aggression.

Other substances

Other substances we ingest have also been linked with anti-social or criminal behaviour. These include food additives and diet, allergens, vitamin deficiencies and lead pollution. They affect various biochemical processes in the body and this in turn can affect behaviour. For example:

- Both lead and the synthetic food colouring tartrazine have been linked with hyperactivity
- Vitamin B deficiency has been linked to erratic and aggressive behaviour.

However, the link between such substances and criminality is not always clear.

ACTIVITY Research

Serotonin   Go to www.criminology.uk.net

NOW TEST YOURSELF

Practice Questions

1. Describe **one** genetic theory of criminality.   (6 marks)
   Source: WJEC Criminology Unit 2 examination 2020
2. Describe **one** physiological theory of criminality.   (6 marks)
   Source: WJEC Criminology Unit 2 examination 2018

Advice

For Question 1, note that genetic theories believe some people inherit genes that make them more likely to commit crime. You could describe the work of Christiansen (twin studies) or Mednick (adoption studies). Describe how twin studies aim to see if monozygotic twins have a higher criminality concordance rate than dizygotic twins. Describe how adoption studies aim to see if adopted children share the level of criminality of their genetic rather than their adoptive parents.

For Question 2, note that these theories believe criminals have distinctive physical features. Use Lombroso or Sheldon's theory. Note how Lombroso claimed to be scientific, that criminality was heritable, that criminals had distinct physical features and were atavistic 'throwbacks' to a more primitive stage. For Sheldon, include his three somatotypes. Describe their physical features, how these link to personality and why mesomorphs were supposedly more likely to be criminals.

Describe individualistic theories of criminality

Getting started

Some theorists argue that criminals have a certain type of personality. Working in small groups, discuss the following questions and then share your answers with the class.

1. What type or types of personality do you think criminals might have?

2. Do different types of offender (e.g. burglars, sex offenders, conmen, serial killers etc.) have particular personality types?

3. Are offenders born with a personality that causes them to offend? Or do they acquire it from their upbringing and environment?

In this Topic, we shall look at the following individualistic theories of criminality:

1. **Psychodynamic theories**, such as psychoanalysis
2. **Eysenck's personality theory**
3. **Learning theories**, such as Bandura's social learning theory
4. **Cognitive theories** of crime.

Psychodynamic theories

Psychodynamic theories see our personality as containing active forces that cause us to act as we do. These forces are powerful urges, feelings and conflicts within the unconscious mind. Criminal behaviour is the result of an individual's failure to resolve these inner conflicts in a socially acceptable way.

Psychoanalysis

The first and most important psychodynamic theory is psychoanalysis, originally founded by Sigmund Freud (1856-1939). According to Freud, our early childhood experiences determine our personality and future behaviour; in his view, 'the child is father to the man'. In particular, our early experiences determine whether we will go on to act in anti-social ways.

According to Freud, the human personality contains three elements: the ego, id and superego. These elements are in tension with one another.

The id is located in the unconscious, instinctive, 'animal' part of the mind. It contains powerful, selfish, pleasure-seeking needs and drives, such as the desire for sex, food and sleep. The id is governed by 'the pleasure principle' – the blind desire to satisfy its urges at any cost. If we acted on these urges whenever we felt them, they would often lead to anti-social and criminal behaviour.

The superego contains our conscience or moral rules, which we learn through interactions with our parents during early socialisation in the family. For example, we may be punished for trying to satisfy our urges without regard for others.

Through socialisation, the child internalises its parents' ideas of right and wrong, and the superego develops as a sort of internal 'nagging parent'. If we act – or even just think of acting – contrary to the superego, it punishes us with feelings of guilt and anxiety.

The ego Freud saw our behaviour as the result of the struggle between the id and the superego. Literally, 'ego' means 'I': I am pulled in opposing directions, between my desires (id) and my conscience (superego). The ego's role is to try to strike a balance between their conflicting demands.

The ego is driven by 'the reality principle': it learns from experience that in the real world, our actions have consequences. For example, a child learns that snatching a biscuit without asking may lead to punishment. The ego seeks to control the id's urges while still finding ways to satisfy them.

For example, a child learns to say 'please' to obtain what it wants. It learns that sometimes it may have to repress gratification of the id's desires. In a well-adjusted person, the ego acts in a way that satisfies the id's desires but that is also morally acceptable to the superego.

Id, ego and superego badges on sale at the Freud Museum, London

---

ACTIVITY Media

Id, ego and superego

Go to www.criminology.uk.net

How does this relate to crime? Psychoanalytic theories see anti-social behaviour as caused by an abnormal relationship with parents during early socialisation, for example due to neglect or to excessively lax or strict parenting. This can result in a weak, over-harsh or deviant superego:

- **A weakly developed superego** means the individual will feel less guilt about anti-social actions and less inhibition about acting on the id's selfish or aggressive urges.
- **A too harsh and unforgiving superego** creates deep-seated guilt feelings in the individual, who then craves punishment as a release from these feelings. The person may engage in compulsive repeat offending in order to be punished.
- **A deviant superego** is one where the child is successfully socialised, but into a deviant moral code. A son may have a perfectly good relationship with his criminal father and so he internalises his father's criminal values. As a result, his superego would not inflict guilt feelings on him for contemplating criminal acts.

> **Question**
> How far do you agree that our early experiences in the family shape our personalities and future behaviour? Give your reasons.

Bowlby's maternal deprivation theory

Freud's ideas have influenced many other theories. Probably the best known of these is Bowlby's maternal deprivation theory.

Bowlby argues that there is a link between maternal deprivation and deviant or anti-social behaviour. In his view, a child needs a close, continuous relationship with its primary carer (which Bowlby assumed would be the mother) from birth to the age of 5 in order to develop normally.

If the mother-child attachment is broken through separation, even for a short period, it can leave the child unable to form meaningful emotional relationships with others. Bowlby describes this as 'affectionless psychopathy'. In some cases, this can lead to criminal behaviour.

Evidence Bowlby based his theory on a study of 44 juvenile thieves who had been referred to a child guidance clinic. He found that 39% of them had suffered maternal deprivation before the age of 5, compared with only 5% of a control group of non-delinquents.

Eysenck's personality theory

Hans Eysenck developed a theory of criminality based on his theory of personality. He argues that criminality is the result of a particular personality type.

For Eysenck, our personality is made up of two dimensions:

- **Extraversion versus introversion** (E for short).
- **Neuroticism versus emotional stability** (N for short).

Extraverted personalities are outgoing, sociable, excitement-seeking, impulsive, carefree, optimistic, often aggressive, short-tempered and unreliable.

Introverted personalities are reserved, inward-looking, thoughtful, serious, quiet, self-controlled, pessimistic and reliable.

Neurotic personalities are anxious, moody, often depressed and prone to over-reacting – whereas emotionally stable personalities are calm, even-tempered, controlled and unworried.

Question

Perhaps introverts are just as likely to commit crimes as extraverts, but less likely to get caught. How would you explain this?

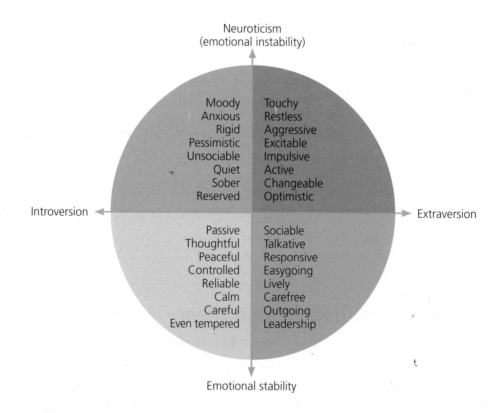

ACTIVITY Research

The Eysenck Personality Questionnaire   Go to www.criminology.uk.net

Eysenck devised the Eysenck Personality Questionnaire to measure people's personality traits, ranking them on an E scale and an N scale. For example, people with a high E score are very extraverted, whereas people with a low E score are very introverted.

Eysenck found that most people have personalities somewhere around the middle on both scales. By contrast, the criminal personality scores high on both E and N. In other words, criminals tend to be strongly extraverted and neurotic.

Why is this? Eysenck explains his findings by drawing on two ideas: conditioning, and genetic inheritance.

Conditioning Some psychologists argue that through experience, we learn to seek pleasure (or rewards) and avoid pain (or punishment). For example, if we misbehave, we are punished and so we learn to stop doing it so as to avoid further punishment. This process is called 'conditioning'.

Eysenck argues that we learn through conditioning, but that some individuals inherit a nervous system that causes them to develop a criminal personality. He argues that this works as follows.

- **Extraverts** have a nervous system that needs a high level of stimulation from their environment, so they are constantly seeking excitement. This leads to impulsive, rule-breaking behaviour. In turn, this is likely to lead to punishment.

- **Neurotics** are harder to condition into following society's rules because their high anxiety levels prevent them learning from punishment for their mistakes.

Thus, the combination of high E and high N is likely to lead to criminality.

Psychoticism In his later research, Eysenck added psychoticism (P) as a further personality dimension. People with a high P score are more likely to engage in criminality. They tend to be solitary misfits who are cruel, insensitive, aggressive and lacking in empathy. High P can overlap with serious psychiatric illnesses such as schizophrenia.

Learning theories

Learning theories of crime generally emphasise three key features:

- Criminal behaviour is *learned* behaviour.
- The influence of our immediate social environment, such as the family and peer groups.
- The key role of reinforcement and punishment in the learning process.

Sutherland's differential association theory

Edwin Sutherland argues that individuals learn criminal behaviour largely in the family and peer groups (including work groups). It is the result of two factors:

Imitation of criminal acts: individuals can acquire criminal skills and techniques through observing those around them.

Learned attitudes Socialisation within the group exposes the individual to attitudes and values about the law. Some of these may be favourable to the law and others unfavourable. If the individual internalises more unfavourable than favourable attitudes and values, they are more likely to become criminals.

For example, in his study of white collar crime, Sutherland found that group attitudes in the workplace often normalised criminal behaviour (e.g. by claiming that 'everyone's doing it'). This made it easier for individual members to justify their own criminal behaviour.

Question

Apart from the idea that 'everyone's doing it', what other justifications might criminals give for their behaviour?

Operant learning theory

Operant learning theory is the work of the psychologist B.F. Skinner. Its basic idea is that if a particular behaviour results in a reward, it is likely to be repeated. On the other hand, behaviour that results in an undesirable outcome is likely not to be repeated. The first kind of behaviour has been positively reinforced, while the second has been punished.

Behaviourism The cause of someone's behaviour lies in the reinforcements and punishments that shape it. This focus on behaviour-shaping has led to operant learning theory becoming known as behaviourism.

Differential reinforcement theory Skinner argues that all behaviour is the result of reinforcements and punishments. If so, then this must explain *criminal* behaviour too. An example of this approach is Jeffery's differential reinforcement theory.

Jeffery argues that criminal behaviour is learned through the reinforcement of particular behaviours. If crime has more rewarding consequences than punishing ones for an individual, they will be more likely to engage in criminal behaviour. These rewards could be financial, but also emotional (e.g. friendship or the respect of peers). If we want to explain someone's offending, we need to look at the balance of rewards and punishments for the particular individual.

ACTIVITY / Media

Operant conditioning   Go to www.criminology.uk.net

Social learning theory

The psychologist Albert Bandura argues that we learn much of our behaviour – including aggressive behaviour – by imitating other people. For this reason, his approach is known as observational or *social* learning theory.

Models Bandura calls these other people 'models', because we model our behaviour on how we see them behaving. However, we don't copy just anybody's behaviour. For example, we are more likely to imitate the model's behaviour if they are of a higher status than us.

Even then, whether we imitate their behaviour mainly depends on the *consequences* of that behaviour. If we see the model being rewarded for their behaviour, we are more likely to imitate it than if we see them being punished for it.

Bandura et al demonstrated this in a series of experiments with 4-5 year olds. They divided the children into three groups. All three were then shown a film of an adult model being verbally and physically aggressive towards an inflatable Bobo doll.

- **Group 1** saw a version of the film where the model was rewarded with praise.
- **Group 2** saw a version in which the model was punished (told off).
- **Group 3** was a control group. In the version they saw, the behaviour was neither rewarded nor punished.

Later, they were left to play with the doll. Group 1 imitated the aggressive behaviours they had seen being rewarded. Group 3, the control group, also imitated the model, though less so. Group 2, who had observed the model being punished, were the least likely to imitate the aggressive behaviour.

Therefore, whether they imitated the behaviour depended on the consequences they had observed for the model. They learned by observing someone else's experience.

This can be applied to criminal behaviour. If an individual observes a model (e.g. a peer) getting rewarded for their criminality, the theory predicts that the behaviour is more likely to be imitated.

Cognitive theories of crime

The term 'cognition' refers to thinking and mental processes such as attitudes, beliefs, reasoning, problem-solving, decision-making, our self-concept and how we interpret the world around us. Cognitive theories argue that these mental processes shape our behaviour. For example, how we interpret a situation affects how we respond to it. Thought processes also affect our emotions; if we interpret a situation as threatening, it may trigger feelings of fear or anger.

Criminal personality theory

Psychologists Yochelson and Samenow have applied cognitive theory to criminality. Their key idea is that criminals are prone to faulty thinking and this makes them more likely to commit crime. Their criminal personality theory is based on a long-term study of 240 male offenders, most of whom had been committed to psychiatric hospital.

Thinking errors They argue that criminals show a range of errors and biases in their thinking and decision-making. These include lying; secretiveness; need for power and control; super-optimism; failure to understand other's positions; lack of trust in others; uniqueness (the feeling that they are special) and the victim stance (blaming others and seeing themselves as the victim). These errors and biases lead the individual to commit crime.

Kohlberg's moral development theory

This is a theory of how we develop our moral thinking. As such it is potentially relevant to understanding criminals' thinking.

Kohlberg argues that our ideas of right and wrong develop through a series of levels and stages from childhood to adulthood. At the 'pre-conventional' or pre-moral level, young children define right and wrong simply in terms of what brings punishment or rewards, whereas by adulthood, our ideas of right and wrong involve an understanding of underlying moral principles and values.

This suggests that criminals' moral development is stuck at a less mature level than everyone else's. They are likely to think solely in terms of whether their actions will lead to a reward or punishment, rather than how it might affect others. This makes them more likely to offend.

Cognitive behavioural therapy Cognitive theories that see delinquents' thought patterns as different from those of normal people have led to a range of treatments for offenders. These come under the general heading of cognitive behavioural therapy. We deal with these in Topic 4.1.

NOW TEST YOURSELF

Practice Question

Describe any **one** individualistic theory of criminality. (6 marks)

Source: WJEC Criminology Unit 2 examination 2017

Answer by Mo

Eysenck's individualistic (psychological) theory argues that criminality is caused by a particular personality type. He sees personalities as made up of two dimensions: extraversion versus introversion and neuroticism versus emotional stability.

Extraverts have excitement-seeking, impulsive, often aggressive personalities. Neurotics are anxious, moody and tend to over-react. Eysenck found that criminals tend to be strongly extraverted and neurotic.

Eysenck explains this in terms of conditioning and genetic inheritance. This is because extraverts genetically inherit a nervous system that needs high levels of stimulation, so they are constantly seeking excitement, which leads them to take risks and break laws, leading to punishment.

However, because criminals tend to be neurotics with high anxiety levels, this prevents their behaviour being conditioned by punishment – they don't learn from the experience and so they continue offending.

Eysenck includes a third personality aspect, psychoticism. Psychotics are cruel, insensitive misfits who lack empathy and are often schizophrenic.

> Good to introduce these key terms at the start.

> Clear description of the two personality types linked to criminality.

> Shows how extraversion leads to offending.

> Understands why criminals are less likely to be successfully conditioned and go on offending.

> A useful brief final point.

Overall comments

This is a Band Three (top band) response. Mo shows very good knowledge of Eysenck's ideas, with clear descriptions of the different personality types and use of specialist vocabulary. He explains the role of conditioning and genetic inheritance and then shows how these lead to criminality by extraverted neurotics. He could have said more about psychoticism (e.g. what kinds of crime they might commit) but he has produced an excellent answer.

Describe sociological theories of criminality

Getting started

Working with a partner

1. Discuss and make notes on how you learned right and wrong as a child.

2. Give one example each of a time when you did wrong and what happened to you.

3. How do you think the way in which you are brought up by your parents or carers affects how you behave when you grow up? Might this affect whether you become a criminal?

Sociological theories of criminality

The basic idea behind sociological theories is that social factors play a decisive part in crime. We shall look at the following sociological explanations: functionalist and subcultural theories; interactionism and labelling theory; the Marxist theory of crime and law; left and right realist theories of crime; and surveillance theories.

Functionalist and subcultural theories

These are structural theories: they focus on the structure of society and how it is organised. Structural theories look at how equal or unequal a society is, what holds it together and what things cause conflict and division. They see the structure of society as being the underlying cause of crime.

Durkheim's functionalist theory

Functionalists such as Emile Durkheim (1858-1917) see society as a stable structure based on shared norms, values and beliefs about right and wrong. This produces social solidarity or integration, where all members of society feel they belong to the same harmonious unit. Most people conform to society's shared norms and do not deviate.

Crime is inevitable

Nevertheless, some crime is inevitable, because in every society some individuals are inadequately socialised and likely to deviate. Society also contains many social groups, each with different values, so shared rules of behaviour become less clear. Durkheim calls this 'anomie' (normlessness) – where shared norms become weakened.

The functions of crime

According to Durkheim, crime in fact performs important functions:

1. **Boundary maintenance** Crime produces a reaction that unites society's members against the wrongdoer, reminding them of the boundary between right and wrong, and reaffirming their shared rules.

2. **Social change** For society to progress, individuals with new ideas must challenge existing norms and values, and at first this will be seen as deviance.

   For example, Nelson Mandela was jailed in South Africa for opposing apartheid (racial segregation), but eventually apartheid was overthrown and Mandela was elected South Africa's first Black president in 1994.

3. **Safety valve** For example, Davis argues that prostitution acts to release men's sexual frustrations without threatening the nuclear family.

4. **Warning light** Deviance indicates that an institution isn't functioning properly; e.g. high truancy rates could indicate problems with the education system.

In 1963, the future President Mandela was labelled a terrorist by a South African court.

| ACTIVITY | Research |

The functions of crime

Go to www.criminology.uk.net

Merton's strain theory

For Robert K. Merton, the root cause of crime lies in the unequal structure of society. He focuses on the USA but his ideas can also be applied to the UK. American society values 'money success' or wealth as the goal people should pursue and tells them they should achieve this through legitimate means such as hard work at school and in a career.

Blocked opportunities However, not everyone has an equal chance of achieving success legitimately because American society is very unequal. Opportunities for working-class people are often blocked by poverty and inadequate schools. This creates a 'strain' between the goal society says they should achieve and the lack of legitimate means to do so.

For Merton, this causes crime and deviance. Some people (Merton calls them 'conformists') can achieve society's goal legitimately. But for those who cannot, he sees four possible deviant ways of adapting to this strain, based on whether they accept society's goal and/or means:

- **Innovation:** innovators accept the goal but find illegal ways of achieving it by committing utilitarian crimes (ones involving financial gain). They are usually from the lower classes, where legitimate opportunities are blocked.

- **Ritualism:** ritualists give up striving for success. They plod along in a dead-end job.

- **Retreatism:** retreatists are dropouts who reject both goal and means. Merton includes 'vagrants, drunkards and drug addicts'.

- **Rebellion:** rebels reject the existing goals and means, replacing them with new ones with the aim of changing society. Examples include political radicals and alternative cultures such as hippies.

Subcultural theories of crime

Delinquent subcultures are groups whose norms and values are deviant. Subcultural theories apply Merton's idea of a strain between goals and means. Their key idea is that these subcultures enable their members to gain status by illegitimate means.

Albert Cohen: status frustration

Cohen agrees with Merton that deviance results from the lower classes' failure to achieve by legitimate means. However:

- Cohen sees subcultural deviance as a *group* response to failure, not just an individual one.
- He focuses on *non-utilitarian* crimes (ones not for financial gain) such as vandalism.

Cohen notes that most working-class boys end up at the bottom of the school's official status hierarchy. Teachers may regard them as 'thick' and put them in the lower streams. As a result, they suffer from *status frustration* – a feeling of worthlessness.

The subculture offers a solution by providing them with an *alternative status hierarchy* in which they can win respect from their peers through delinquent actions. It inverts society's values (turns them upside down): for example, society respects property, whereas the boys gain status in the group by vandalising property.

Cloward and Ohlin: three subcultures

Cloward and Ohlin note that different neighbourhoods give rise to different types of deviant subcultures:

- **Criminal subcultures** arise in areas where there is a longstanding professional criminal network. They select suitable youths for an 'apprenticeship' in utilitarian crime and a future criminal career.
- **Conflict subcultures** arise where the only criminal opportunities are within street gangs. Violence provides a release for frustration and a source of status earned by winning territory from rival gangs.
- **Retreatist subcultures** are made up of dropouts who have failed in both the legitimate and the illegitimate opportunity structures. They are often based on drug use.

Question

What similarities and differences are there between retreatist subcultures and Merton's idea of retreatism as an adaptation to strain?

Interactionism

Interactionists see our interactions with one another as based on *meanings* or labels. For example, 'criminal' is a label that some people (such as police officers) may attach to others (such as young males) in their interactions with one another. 'Crime' and 'criminals' are social constructs – meanings that we create through our social interactions.

Labelling theory

Labelling theory states that no act is deviant or criminal in itself. It only becomes so when we create rules and apply them to others. For example, the act of smoking cannabis only 'counts' as a crime if society decides to make a law criminalising it and applies that law to cannabis smokers. Therefore to understand criminality, we must focus on how certain actions and people get labelled as criminal in the first place.

Differential enforcement of the law

Interactionists argue that social control agencies such as the police label certain groups as criminal. This results in differential enforcement – where the law is enforced more against one group than against another. Piliavin and Briar found police decisions to arrest were based on stereotypical ideas about a person's manner, dress, gender, class and ethnicity, and the time and place. Young males stopped late at night in high-crime areas were more likely to be arrested.

Canadian flag with cannabis leaf replacing the official maple leaf: part of the campaign to legalise the drug.

Similarly, as we saw in Unit 1, Topic 1.5, Cicourel found that police use typifications (stereotypes) of the 'typical delinquent'. Working-class and ethnic minority youths are more likely to fit the typification and be stopped, arrested and charged.

Labelling and the self-fulfilling prophecy

As Edwin Lemert argues, labelling is a cause of crime and deviance. By labelling certain people as deviant, society encourages them to become more so. He explains this by distinguishing between primary and secondary deviance:

- **Primary deviance** involves acts that have not been publicly labelled. They are often trivial and mostly go uncaught, such as travelling on public transport without paying. Those who commit these acts do not usually see themselves as criminals.

- **Secondary deviance** results from labelling. People may treat the offender solely in terms of his label, which becomes his *master status* or controlling identity. The individual is seen as, say, a thief, overriding all his other statuses, such as father, churchgoer, workmate etc.

As a result, the offender may be rejected by society and forced into the company of other criminals, joining a deviant subculture. Prison is an extreme example of this: the offender is excluded from normal society and placed with others who confirm his criminal identity, provide him with criminal role models and teach him criminal skills.

What has happened is a *self-fulfilling prophecy*: the individual has now become what the label said he was. The result is that further offending becomes more likely.

ACTIVITY / Media

Labelling   Go to www.criminology.uk.net

The deviance amplification spiral

A further example of the interactionist approach is the deviance amplification spiral. This is where the attempt to control deviance through a 'crackdown' leads to it increasing rather than decreasing. This prompts even greater attempts to control it and, in turn, yet more deviance, in an escalating spiral.

Mods and rockers We saw an example of the amplification spiral in Unit 1, Topic 1.5, with Cohen's study of the mods and rockers:

- **Media exaggeration** caused growing public concern.
- **Moral entrepreneurs** called for a 'crackdown'. Police responded by arresting more youths, provoking more concern.
- **Negative labelling** of mods and rockers as 'folk devils' marginalised them further, resulting in more deviance.

The hippies Jock Young's study of hippy cannabis users also found an amplification spiral. Initially, drug use was not central to the hippies' lifestyle and went undetected by the law (primary deviance). However, increased police attention, labelling them as addicts, with raids and arrests, led them to retreat into closed groups. There they developed a deviant subculture where hard drug use was a central activity (self-fulfilling prophecy). This shows how control processes (the police's action) aimed at producing law-abiding behaviour instead produced the opposite.

Interactionism and crime statistics

Interactionists reject the use of the crime statistics compiled by the police. They argue that the statistics measure what the *police* do rather than what *criminals* do.

For example, if the police stereotype working-class males as typical criminals, they will spend more time pursuing this group than middle-class white collar criminals. As a result, the statistics will be full of working-class males, simply because of the police's stereotypes. Their statistics are therefore just a social construction, not a true measure of the amount of crime.

The Marxist theory of crime and law

Marxism is a structural theory. Marxists argue that the unequal structure of capitalist society shapes people's behaviour. This includes criminal behaviour and how society deals with it.

Marxists argue that capitalist society is divided into two classes:

- **the ruling capitalist class** or *bourgeoisie,* who own the means of production (businesses, banks, land etc.)
- **the working class** or *proletariat*, whose labour the capitalists exploit to make profit.

All the institutions of capitalist society work to maintain this inequality and exploitation. This is especially true of the law and criminal justice system. For Marxists, the law and its enforcement by the courts and police are simply a means of keeping the working class in their place.

The Marxist view of crime and the law has three main elements: capitalism causes crime; law making and law enforcement are biased; and crime and the law perform ideological functions.

Capitalism causes crime

For Marxists, crime is inevitable in capitalist society, because capitalism is a *criminogenic* (crime-causing) system. This is due to several reasons:

- The exploitation of the working class drives many people into poverty, meaning crime may be the only way to survive.
- Capitalism continually pushes consumer goods at people through advertising, resulting in utilitarian crimes (e.g. theft) to obtain them.
- Inequality causes feelings of alienation and frustration, resulting in non-utilitarian crimes (e.g. violence and vandalism).
- Capitalism causes crime among the capitalists themselves. Capitalism is a dog-eat-dog system and the profit motive promotes greed. This encourages capitalists to commit corporate crimes (e.g. tax evasion, breaking health and safety laws) to gain an advantage.

Making and enforcing the law

Marxists see both law making and law enforcement as serving the interests of the capitalist class.

Law making William Chambliss argues that the laws are made to protect the private property of the rich. For example, there are laws against the homeless squatting empty houses, but no laws against the rich owning several houses. Very few laws challenge the unequal distribution of wealth.

> **Question**
> What laws could be introduced to distribute wealth more equally?

Selective law enforcement Marxists agree with interactionists that the law is enforced selectively – against the working class but not the upper classes. White collar and corporate crimes of the rich are much less likely to be prosecuted than working-class 'street' crimes:

- Out of 200 companies who had broken safety laws, Carson found that only three were prosecuted.
- Despite the large number of deaths at work caused by employers' negligence, there was only one successful prosecution of a UK firm in eight years for corporate homicide.
- Corporate crime is often punished less severely, for example with fines rather than jail – even though it often causes great harm.

Ideological functions of crime and the law

Marxists argue that ideas about crime and the law are an *ideology* – a set of ideas that conceal the inequality of capitalist society. For example:

- Selective enforcement makes it look as if crime is the fault of the working class. This divides the working class, encouraging workers to blame working-class criminals for their problems, rather than capitalism.
- This also shifts attention away from much more serious ruling-class crime.
- Some laws do benefit workers to a limited extent, e.g. health and safety laws. However, Pearce argues that these also benefit capitalism by giving it a 'caring' face.

These ideas encourage the working class to accept capitalism instead of replacing it with a more equal society.

Right realism and crime

Right realists have a right wing, conservative political outlook. They see crime, especially street crime, as a growing problem. Right realists are mainly concerned with practical solutions to reduce crime. In their view, the best way to do so is through control and punishment, rather than by rehabilitating offenders or tackling causes such as poverty.

The causes of crime

Right realists reject the Marxist view that factors such as poverty are the cause of crime. Instead, they argue that crime is the product of three factors: biological differences between individuals; inadequate socialisation; and offending is a rational choice.

Biological differences between individuals

According to Wilson and Herrnstein, biological differences make some individuals more likely to commit crime. In their view, personality traits associated with criminality, such as aggressiveness, risk-taking or low intelligence, are innate (inborn).

Inadequate socialisation

Effective socialisation can reduce the chances of someone offending by teaching them self-control and correct values. Right realists see the nuclear family as the best agency of socialisation.

However, according to Murray, the nuclear family is being undermined by generous welfare benefits. He claims that this has led to a steady rise in the number of welfare-dependent lone parent families. Fathers no longer need to remain in the home and take responsibility for supporting their families, since the state does it for them.

The underclass Murray argues that welfare dependency is creating an 'underclass' who fail to socialise their children properly. Absent fathers mean that boys lack discipline and an appropriate male role model, because they do not see a man who works hard to support his family. As a result, boys turn to delinquent role models in street gangs and young men gain status through crime rather than through supporting their families.

Offending is a rational choice

An important part of right realism is *rational choice theory* (RCT). This assumes that we are rational beings with free will. Deciding to commit a crime is a choice based on a rational calculation of the consequences: basically, weighing the risks/costs against the rewards/benefits. If the rewards of crime appear to outweigh the risks, people will be more likely to offend.

Right realists argue that the crime rate is high because the perceived costs of crime are low. Criminals see little risk of being caught and do not expect to receive severe punishments even if they are convicted.

Felson's routine activity theory puts forward a similar idea. He argues that for a crime to occur, three factors are necessary: (i) a motivated offender, (ii) a suitable target (a victim or property) and (iii) the absence of a 'capable guardian' (e.g. a police officer or neighbour). Felson sees offenders as acting rationally, which is why the presence of a guardian is likely to deter them.

However, one problem is that if RCT is correct, offenders may act rationally and just move their attention to where the target is softer. This is called displacement – crime doesn't decline, it just moves.

Question
Why might right realism be better at explaining crimes such as burglary or shoplifting than violent crimes such as assault?

Left realism and crime

Left realists have a left wing, socialist political outlook. They see inequality in capitalist society as the root cause of crime. They argue that the main victims are disadvantaged groups: the working class, ethnic minorities and women. Crime rates are highest in working-class areas with high levels of unemployment and deprivation. There is also evidence that the police take crimes against these groups less seriously. Left realists propose to reduce crime by making society fairer and more equal.

The causes of crime

Lea and Young identify three related causes of crime: relative deprivation, subculture and marginalisation.

Relative deprivation

For left realists, crime has its roots in relative deprivation – how deprived or badly off someone feels *in relation to others*. Lea and Young argue that two factors are increasing people's sense of relative deprivation:

- On the one hand, the media continually pump out messages urging everyone to aspire to material possessions, promoting what Young calls 'a culture hooked on Gucci, BMW, Nikes'.
- On the other hand, society is becoming more unequal due to cuts in benefits, unemployment, job insecurity and low pay.

At one extreme, many people now have no chance of ever affording the sort of lifestyle the media portray. At the other extreme, footballers, 'fat cat' bankers and others receive what many regard as undeservedly high rewards. Due to this perceived unfairness, some resort to crime to obtain what they feel should be rightfully theirs.

Question

What similarities can you see with Merton's ideas of money success, blocked opportunities and strain?

Young notes that there is now also 'relative deprivation downwards': people who are better off feel resentment against those who are actually worse off, who they see as scroungers. This may explain some hate crimes against powerless groups, for example asylum seekers or the disabled.

Subculture

For left realists, a subculture is a group's way of solving the problem of relative deprivation. Some subcultures turn to crime to solve the problem.

Criminal subcultures share society's materialistic goals, but because legitimate opportunities are blocked (for example, they are denied access to well paid jobs), they resort to crime. Inner city youths may find they are denied access to well paid jobs, because of discrimination or the poor quality of education they have received. Crime then becomes an alternative means of achieving the consumer goods they desire.

However, not all subcultures turn to crime. Some may turn to religion instead to find comfort and an explanation for their deprivation (e.g. that it is God's will). This may encourage conformity rather than criminality.

Marginalisation

According to Lea and Young, marginalised groups are ones that lack organisations to represent their interests and lack clearly defined goals. For example, unemployed youth are a highly marginalised group.

Unlike workers, who have clear goals (e.g. better wages) and organisations to give voice to their grievances (such as trade unions), jobless youths have no clear goals or organisations to represent them. Instead, they have a sense of powerlessness, frustration and resentment of injustice, which they express through crime such as violence and rioting.

Surveillance theories

Surveillance involves monitoring people to control crime. Surveillance theories look at the methods by which surveillance is carried out, including technology such as CCTV, tagging and databases that produce profiles of individuals and groups.

Foucault: the Panopticon

Foucault argues that in modern society, we are increasingly controlled through self-surveillance, through what he calls 'disciplinary power'. He illustrates this by reference to a prison design known as the Panopticon (meaning 'all-seeing').

In the Panopticon, prisoners' cells are visible to the guards from a central viewing point (e.g. a watchtower) but prisoners cannot see the guards. Therefore, not knowing if they are being watched, the prisoners must constantly behave as if they are. In this way, surveillance turns into self-surveillance and discipline becomes self-discipline: control is invisible, inside the prisoner's own mind.

Foucault argues that other institutions (e.g. mental hospitals, army barracks, workplaces and schools) have followed this pattern. Disciplinary power and self-surveillance has now infiltrated every part of society and reaches every individual.

ACTIVITY / Media

Foucault   Go to www.criminology.uk.net

How many CCTV cameras are monitoring *your* behaviour?

Synoptic surveillance

Mathiesen argues that as well as surveillance from above, as in the Panopticon, we now have surveillance from below. He calls this the 'Synopticon' – where everybody watches everybody.

For example, motorists and cyclists can monitor the behaviour of others by using dashboard or helmet cameras. This may warn other road users that they are under surveillance and result in them exercising self-discipline.

> **Question**
> What other situations can you think of where you are either being monitored or you are monitoring others?

Actuarial justice and profiling

The term 'actuarial' comes from the insurance industry; an actuary is someone who calculates the risk of certain events happening. For example, what is the likelihood of your home being burgled in the next 12 months?

Feeley and Simon see actuarial justice as a new form of surveillance. Its aim is to predict and prevent future offending. It uses statistical information to reduce crime by compiling profiles of likely offenders.

NOW TEST YOURSELF

Practice Question

Briefly describe **one** sociological theory of criminality. (4 marks)

Source: WJEC Criminology Unit 2 examination 2020

Advice

Choose one of the following sociological theories of criminality: Durkheim's functionalist theory; Merton's strain theory; subcultural theory; labelling theory; Marxism; right realism; left realism; surveillance theories (e.g. Foucault).

Whichever theory you choose, make sure you include some of its key terms and build your answer around them. For example:

For subcultural theory: group response to failure; status frustration; alternative status hierarchy; non-utilitarian crime; criminal, conflict and retreatist subcultures.

For labelling theory: crime is a social construct; differential enforcement of the law; police stereotyping; the self-fulfilling prophecy; primary and secondary deviance; master status; the deviance amplification spiral.

For other theories, look back through this Topic and make a list of the key terms of each theory to use in your answer.

This is a short question and it would be good practice to write two or more answers, each one about a different sociological theory.

Analyse situations of criminality

Getting started

Working on your own

1. Write one sentence on each of three different biological explanations of why people commit crime.

2. Now do the same for three individualistic and three sociological theories of crime.

Now share your answers with the class and note any points you did not have.

The previous three Topics looked at theories that aim to explain criminality. In this Topic, we shall apply these theories to some case studies dealing with particular situations of criminality. Some of the case studies are drawn from real life, while others are scenarios similar to ones that you could be given in the Unit 2 examination.

Eddie's case

Eddie is 13. He is doing badly in school and has been put in the bottom set for most subjects. Teachers regard Eddie as a bit 'thick'. They either ignore him or they discipline him when he can't follow the lesson and starts misbehaving to amuse his mates, or just to relieve the boredom. He dislikes school and feels the teachers look down on him. He knows he's going to fail and can't wait to leave.

Eddie hangs out with other boys who share his dislike of school. They often truant together and hang around the shopping centre, where they have got to know some older boys, one of whom is called Tony. Tony is full of bravado; he was recently convicted of minor vandalism offences and likes to brag about it. Eddie and the others are impressed and see Tony's criminal record as a badge of honour.

Eddie would like to be like Tony because all Eddie's friends look up to Tony as a sort of leader. Eddie decides to get a can of paint and sprays graffiti on the school's wall.

Applying theories to Eddie's case

We can apply sociological explanations to Eddie's case, including labelling and subcultural theories, as well as individualistic approaches like social learning theory.

Labelling theory

Eddie's teachers labelled him as 'thick' and the school placed him in the bottom sets, suggesting they have a low opinion of him and expect him to fail. This has become a self-fulfilling prophecy – Eddie has accepted the school's view of him as a failure: he doesn't like school (after all, school doesn't much like him); he gets bored, misbehaves, gets in trouble and truants. Educational failure is often linked to criminal behaviour and may be the underlying cause of Eddie's criminality.

Subcultural theory

Cohen's subcultural theory states that working-class boys underachieve and are denied status at school (for example, by being put in bottom sets like Eddie). To compensate, they seek status by joining a deviant subculture with boys in a similar situation (Eddie's truanting friends). The subculture inverts mainstream society's values. For example, society values respect for property but the subculture shows contempt for property by committing acts of vandalism, as both Eddie and Tony do. Such acts gain boys status in the subculture's alternative status hierarchy: Tony's criminal conviction was a badge of honour, not shame, and the others look up to him.

Social learning theory

This states that if we observe a model's behaviour being positively reinforced, we are more likely to imitate it. Eddie sees Tony being rewarded by the other boys who are impressed by his criminal behaviour and decides to imitate him by spraying graffiti. Imitation is more likely if the model is someone of higher status but who the imitator can identify with: Tony makes a good model because he is a bit older but easy to identify with because in other respects he is in a similar position to Eddie.

The case of the Ford Pinto

From the 1970s, the Ford Motor Company in the USA was facing growing competition from Japanese and European small car manufacturers. Lee Iacocca, head of Ford, called for the company to produce a small car costing less than $2,000. To meet these requirements, the designers put the fuel tank in the rear end of the new car, the Pinto.

Although the Pinto's design complied with government car safety regulations, Ford's own tests showed that the fuel tank was vulnerable to bursting into flames when the car was involved in rear-end collisions. Ford conducted a cost-benefit analysis to calculate the harm likely to result from this defect. They estimated that there would be 180 deaths and 180 serious burns injuries (skin graft level), plus 2,100 burned out cars. Ford calculated that it would be cheaper to pay compensation for the deaths and injuries ($49m in total) than to redesign the car and fix the problem, which amounted to $11 per car ($137m in total).

In 1978, Ford were prosecuted for criminal negligence following the death of three schoolgirls when a Pinto caught fire following a rear-end collision. However, the company was acquitted – a fact the prosecutor attributed to Ford's enormous legal resources, which enabled it to keep much critical evidence out of the trial.

ACTIVITY / Media

Corporate crime 1

Go to www.criminology.uk.net

Applying theories to the Pinto case

Sociological theories such as strain theory, right realism and Marxism have been applied to the case of the Ford Pinto.

Strain theory

Merton's strain theory is usually used to explain working-class crime, but it can be applied to corporate crime as well. Merton argued that American culture values material wealth or 'money success' and those who cannot obtain it by legitimate means will tend to adopt illegitimate ones instead – which Merton calls 'innovation'.

In Ford's case, their profits were being squeezed by foreign competition and so to hold on to their market, they produced a cheap car, even while knowing of the fire risks. They also chose to pay out compensation for death and injury rather than spend the additional $11 per car to make it safer.

Right realism

The right realists' rational choice theory can be applied to the case. The theory states that criminals weigh up the risks and rewards, or costs and benefits, before deciding whether to commit a crime. Ford's cost-benefit analysis indicated that it would be cheaper, and therefore rational from the point of view of its profits, to pay compensation rather than fix the defect.

ACTIVITY / **Applying Marxist theory to the Ford Pinto case**

Working with a partner

1. Look back at Topic 2.3 to remind yourself of the Marxist view of crime and the law.

2. In what ways could Marxist ideas about crime and the law be applied to the case of the Ford Pinto?

Simon's case

Simon is an opportunistic thief and a conman, though not always a successful one. As a thief, he is always on the look-out for the opportunity to snatch something quickly when the security guard is distracted and isn't paying attention, or when he spots a parked car with its window open and a bag left on the seat.

Simon is a repeat offender. He is very sociable and can be quite charming, but he has a high opinion of himself; he is cocky, self-confident and egotistical. He has no sympathy for the victims that he cons and he thinks they are mugs who 'had it coming': it's their own fault. Simon had a deprived childhood and he is scathing about well-off people who 'don't know they're born'. 'They deserve everything they get – and then some', he says.

Simon only thinks about whether he can get away with something, not whether it would be immoral. 'In this world,' he says, 'it's every man for himself. You've got to look after number one.' However, he tends to get caught because he's not very good at working out his chances of getting away with the crime. He is too impulsive and restless to think things through carefully, over-optimistic about his chances of success, enjoys taking the risks and minimises the obstacles.

Applying theories to Simon's case

We can apply several individualistic and sociological theories to Simon's case.

Cognitive theories

Yochelson and Samenow's criminal personality theory argues that criminality is the result of errors and biases in criminals' thought processes, including egotism, super-optimism, uniqueness (having a very high opinion of oneself), victim-blaming and lying. These are all characteristics of Simon's personality. These errors lead to criminal behaviour: it is easier to commit a crime if, like Simon, you believe that victims deserve what they get.

Kohlberg's moral development theory argues that some individuals are stuck at the 'pre-conventional' or pre-moral stage found in young children. In this stage, the individual defines right and wrong simply in terms of what brings rewards or punishments. Simon is stuck at this stage; he believes that if you can get away with something, then it's acceptable, regardless of its consequences for others.

Eysenck's personality theory

Eysenck argues that criminality is the result of an extraverted-neurotic personality type. Extraverts are impulsive, sociable, optimistic, excitement-seeking risk-takers – all traits that Simon has. Their constant quest for excitement often lands them in trouble with the law. Neurotics have high anxiety levels that make it harder to condition them through punishment, so they don't learn from their mistakes. Simon is a repeat offender who presumably has not learned from his previous punishments.

Right realism

Routine activity theory states that criminals are opportunists who offend when their 'target' (the things Simon steals from shops and cars) lacks a 'capable guardian' (for example, when the security guard isn't looking). Similarly, rational choice theory argues that offenders weigh up risk versus reward to decide whether to offend. Simon tries to do this, though he is too impulsive and optimistic to make fully rational choices and so he often gets caught.

Marxism

Marxism sees criminality as a product of capitalism, which is based on class conflict. Simon comes from a deprived background and he shows a sort of class consciousness in his attitude to his well-off victims, who seem like a class enemy. Marxists would also argue that Simon's selfishness ('looking after number one') is unsurprising: capitalism breeds a competitive, dog-eat-dog mentality.

Darren's case

Darren is 18. He went to a 'failing' school, left with very few qualifications and now works as a scaffolder in his uncle's firm, where he has been helping out since he was 13. Unfortunately it's insecure casual work, not regular employment. Darren is a big young man – the work is heavy and has built up his muscles. It can be dangerous, too. Once, when he was 14, he was struck on the head by a scaffolding pole, but he's tough and didn't go to hospital.

Darren looks tough, too, and lately this has started to lead others to 'have a go' at him in pubs and clubs. He has become short-tempered and tends to react aggressively to provocation. He is beginning to get a bit of a reputation. The police have been called on a couple of these occasions. They tend to see Darren as a bit of a 'hard case' and put the blame on him even when he hasn't started the fight.

Darren often finds himself a bit short of money. He likes the branded clothing and footwear that he sees advertised everywhere and he has taken to occasional shoplifting to get the latest fashions.

Branded sportswear: desirable but expensive. Stealing may be the only way some can get it.

Applying theories to Darren's case

Several sociological theories of criminality can be applied to Darren's case, including the following.

Labelling theory

Darren has gained a reputation for his temper and the police have labelled him a 'hard case' and see him as a troublemaker. This might be partly due to his physique, which may give the idea that he can 'handle' himself. This may make them more likely to arrest and charge him and could ultimately become a self-fulfilling prophecy. As a young working-class male, he also fits their typification or stereotype of the 'typical criminal'.

Left realism

Left realists could explain Darren's shoplifting in terms of relative deprivation. He sees advertisements for desirable consumer goods but doesn't earn much in his insecure manual job and so he resorts to crime.

Strain theory

Merton's theory would take a similar view. Attending a failing school would probably have blocked his access to legitimate opportunities such as good qualifications and a well-paid job. He therefore 'innovates' by using shoplifting to obtain socially desirable goods.

Marxism

Like strain theory and left realism, Marxism takes a structural view. Capitalism needs and encourages people to consume what it produces in order to make profits, but Darren's position in the class structure of capitalist society means his only way of obtaining these goods is through crime.

ACTIVITY / **Applying biological theories to Darren's case**

Working with a partner

1. Look back at Topic 2.1 to remind yourself of biological theories of criminality.
2. In what ways could biological theories be applied to Darren's case?

The case of the Enron Corporation

At its height, Enron was the seventh largest company in the United States. It engaged in a variety of illegal practices, including concealing its debts and publishing false information about its profits, with the aim of boosting its share price, which rose by about 1000% between 1990 and 2000. But by the end of 2001 the share price had collapsed from $90.75 to 26 cents. Enron filed for bankruptcy, with huge losses for shareholders as well as employees, who lost their jobs and whose pension funds were invested in Enron shares.

The chairman Kenneth Lay, chief executive officer Jeffrey Skilling and other senior executives had a vested interest in inflating the share price, since their bonuses came in the form of company shares, which they then sold at the artificially high price, making them hundreds of millions of dollars. Just days before filing for bankruptcy, Enron paid out $55m in bonuses to 500 executives.

Internally, the company culture was one of intense loyalty to the organisation, while externally Enron had an ultra-respectable appearance: Lay gave generously to charity and had top-level political contacts, for example with President George W. Bush. This may have added to the sense within the company that its business practices were legitimate. Many of the worst offenders within the company were greedy, egocentric risk takers with no sense of morality.

Lay was convicted on ten counts of fraud but died before being sentenced. Skilling was sentenced to 14 years in prison for fraud and conspiracy. Meanwhile, shareholders received compensation worth about a tenth of what they had lost; employees only received about $3,000 compensation for their lost pensions - a fraction of what they had paid into the pension fund.

ACTIVITY / Media

Corporate crime 2

Go to www.criminology.uk.net

Applying theories to the Enron case

Sociological and individualistic theories of criminality such as the following have been applied to the case of the Enron executives.

Marxism

Marxists would argue that the naked greed, competitiveness and amorality shown by Lay, Skilling and other executives are a product of the selfish, dog-eat-dog mentality that capitalism encourages. Similarly, their exploitative attitude towards the company's employees (who lost their jobs and pensions) illustrates the conflict of interest between capitalists and workers.

Differential association theory

Sutherland would explain the criminality of the senior executives in terms of the company's internal culture. He argues that individuals may learn criminal behaviour at work, where peer groups socialise them into criminal attitudes and values. Enron's prevailing culture was one of dishonesty which normalised criminality, enabling senior executives to justify their behaviour.

Labelling theory

Labelling theory can be applied to explain the fact that Enron's ultra-respectable public image enabled its bosses to get away with their corrupt practices for so long without being negatively labelled, simply because the company appeared to be above suspicion.

Eysenck

Eysenck's personality theory suggests that Lay, Skilling and the other executives were likely to be extraverts.

Their tendency to indulge in 'casino capitalism' antics, gambling with shareholders' and employees' investments and savings to line their own pockets, and their assumption that the share price would continue to rise indefinitely, match some key characteristics of extraverts: aggression, risk-taking, excitement-seeking and optimism.

Former Enron chief finance officer Andrew Fastow in shackles and handcuffs.

Sharon's case

Sharon was taken into institutional care when she had just turned three. Her home life up to then had been chaotic. Her parents were petty thieves and drug users who neglected both her physical and her emotional needs, and her father was prone to sudden violent outbursts. Her parents had both spent periods away from home; her mother had been in a drug rehabilitation clinic and her father served a prison sentence for dealing. Social workers' reports described Sharon as cold and emotionally withdrawn.

Sharon was eventually placed with foster parents but was unable to bond successfully with them and the relationship soon broke down – a pattern that was repeated several times over the following years. However, she eventually succeeded in forming some sort of relationship with her friend Ellie's family (who were known locally as career criminals) and moved in with them.

At the age of 11 Sharon began abusing various substances, including alcohol, which she says help her to 'escape'. Now 15, she is rarely in school and has been in frequent contact with the youth justice system for a variety of offences including shoplifting (she was caught with Ellie's elder sister, Laura, stealing makeup) and several cases of assault. The neighbourhood has long had high levels of crime, and police and social services are concerned that Sharon is learning the 'tricks of the trade' from her friend's family.

Applying theories to Sharon's case

A range of theories can be applied to help explain different aspects of Sharon's case, such as the following.

Maternal deprivation

Sharon was separated from her parents at an early age when she was taken into care, and prior to that her parents were absent for significant periods. She may have failed to form a successful attachment to either parent. This is supported by the social workers' reports describing her as cold and emotionally withdrawn. This may indicate 'affectionless psychopathy', which Bowlby found in maternally deprived juvenile thieves.

Biological explanations

Given her parents' deviant behaviour, there may be a genetically inherited element in Sharon's own offending, aggression and substance abuse. Biochemical factors such as alcohol could also play a part, since it is known to trigger aggression.

Subcultural theory

This focuses on how individuals may be socialised into a deviant subculture. Sharon's criminality could be explained using Cloward and Ohlin's theory that failure to achieve mainstream goals because of blocked opportunities (she has dropped out of school) may mean she is recruited into a criminal subculture where she can acquire criminal skills. Sharon's involvement with Ellie's family may give her this opportunity (she was caught stealing with Ellie's sister).

Differential association theory

This theory focuses on socialisation in face-to-face groups like the family. If an individual is exposed to values favourable to law-breaking, as Sharon has been both with her parents and Ellie's family, they are more likely to engage in criminal behaviour themselves.

Social learning theory

Bandura argues that we learn behaviour through observing whether others are rewarded or punished for engaging in it. Sharon is likely to have seen Ellie's family reap the rewards of criminal activity and this may have encouraged her to copy them. Social learning theory also stresses the importance of models – individuals whose behaviour we are likely to imitate. Laura, an older girl than Sharon, may have provided such a model.

ACTIVITY — Applying psychoanalysis to Sharon's case

Working with a partner

1. Look back at Topic 2.2 to remind yourself of the psychoanalytic view of criminality.
2. In what ways could psychoanalysis be applied to Sharon's case?

NOW TEST YOURSELF

Scenario

Sammy moved to the city to seek work after losing his job as a welder. He found work that didn't even pay the minimum wage, but was made redundant when the firm went bankrupt. Soon after, his landlord put up the rent and Sammy was evicted when he couldn't pay. He began living on the street, using begging and petty theft to stay alive. He was shunned by respectable society and harassed by the police. His only companions now were other outcasts, some of whom were substance abusers; soon Sammy had a drug habit himself.

Practice Question

Many sociologists have tried to explain criminality. How would (i) Marxism and (ii) any one other sociological theory of criminality that you read about in Topic 2.3 explain Sammy's case?

Advice

Note the key ideas of Marxism and of the other theory you have chosen and see how they could be applied to Sammy's case.

For example, Marxism might focus on how capitalism is based on exploitation (e.g. Sammy's low pay), is criminogenic and causes the poor to commit crime (Sammy's petty theft); how the rich break the law too (paying Sammy below the minimum wage); how the law is selectively enforced (police harassment).

For part (ii), you might want to use the theory that you chose in your answer to the Practice Question at the end of Topic 2.3.

Evaluate the effectiveness of criminological theories to explain causes of criminality

Getting started

Working with a partner, recap Topic 3.1 on how different theories can be used to explain different types of crime. When you have answered the questions below, share your answers with the class to compare responses.

1. Which theory did you find most useful in explaining white collar crime? Give reasons for your answer.

2. Which theory did you find most useful in explaining how family and upbringing can cause criminal behaviour? Give reasons for your answer.

Evaluating theories of criminality

In Topics 2.1, 2.2 and 2.3, we looked at different theories of criminality. In this Topic, we shall evaluate the effectiveness of these theories.

What is evaluation? Evaluating a theory of criminality involves weighing up the arguments and evidence for and against it, and looking at criticisms made from other points of view. We can also ask whether the theory explains all types of criminality, or only some. We should also remember that a theory often has both strengths *and* limitations when it comes to explaining criminality.

Evaluating biological theories

We can group biological theories into four main types: physiological theories, genetic theories, brain injuries and disorders, and biochemical explanations. We shall now evaluate these theories, so you might want to have a quick look back at Topic 2.1 to refresh your memory.

Physiological theories (1) Lombroso

Key idea Lombroso argued that criminals are physically different from non-criminals, for example in terms of their facial characteristics.

Strengths

- Lombroso was the first person to study crime scientifically, using objective measurements to gather evidence. Previously, crime was seen as a moral or religious issue.
- His research showed the importance of examining clinical and historical records of criminals.
- His later work took some limited account of social and environmental factors, not just heredity.
- By arguing that offenders were not freely choosing to commit crime, Lombroso helps us to focus on how we might prevent further offending rather than simply punishing offenders.

Limitations

- Research since Lombroso has failed to show a link between facial features and criminality.

- Lombroso failed to compare his findings on prisoners with a control group of non-criminals. Had he done so, he may have found the same characteristics among the general population; in which case, his explanation would be invalid.

- By describing criminals as like 'primitive savages', Lombroso equates non-western societies with criminals. This is a form of racism.

ACTIVITY / Research

Criticisms of Lombroso   Go to www.criminology.uk.net

Physiological theories (2) Sheldon

Key idea Sheldon argued that somatotype (body type) is related to criminality: mesomorphs are more likely than other types to commit crimes.

Strengths

- Other studies have replicated Sheldon's findings. Glueck and Glueck found that 60% of the offenders in their study were mesomorphs.

- The most serious delinquents in Sheldon's sample were the ones with the most extremely mesomorphic body shapes.

Limitations

- Glueck and Glueck found that criminality was best explained not by biology alone, but by a combination of biological, psychological and environmental factors.

- Criminals may develop a mesomorphic build as a result of needing to be physically tough to succeed. If so, criminality causes somatotype, rather than somatotype causing criminality.

- Social class may be the true cause both of offending and of mesomorphy. Convicted offenders are mainly working-class males, who are more likely to be in manual jobs where they acquire an athletic build.

- Labelling may play a part. Mesomorphs may be labelled as troublemakers because they fit the 'tough guy' stereotype, resulting in a self-fulfilling prophecy. Or they may attract more police attention and get caught more than other somatotypes.

- Sheldon doesn't account for those endomorphs and ectomorphs who do commit crimes. Nor does he explain whether mesomorphs commit crimes other than violence.

> **Question**
> In your opinion, what is the main weakness of physiological theories of criminality?

Genetic theories (1) twin studies

Key idea Genetic theories argue that crime has genetic causes. Identical (MZ) twins are genetically identical, so if one is criminal, we should find that the other is too.

Strengths

- Because MZ twins are genetically identical, it is logical to examine whether their offending behaviour is also identical.

- Twin studies give some support to genetic explanations. Ishikawa and Raine found a higher concordance rate for identical than for non-identical twins. (The concordance rate measures the probability of both twins being criminals, if one of them is.)

Limitations

- If genes were the only cause of criminality, identical twins would show 100% concordance, but studies only show around half or less.

- Higher concordance rates between identical twins may be due to sharing the same home, school etc. Their shared environment might cause similarities in their criminal behaviour, not identical genes.

- Parents treat identical twins more alike than they do non-identical twins. Also, identical twins may feel closer than non-identical twins do, so one twin may be influenced by the other's criminality to become criminal too. These environmental factors may produce similarities in behaviour.

- It is impossible to isolate and measure the effect of genes separately from environmental effects.

- In early studies, there was no way of knowing for certain if twins were in fact genetically identical, since DNA testing did not exist.

Genetic theories (2) adoption studies

Key idea Comparing adopted children's level of criminality with that of both their biological parents and their adoptive parents may allow us to see how far genes influence criminality.

Strengths

- Adoption studies overcome the problem faced by twin studies, where biologically identical twins are brought up in the same household, which makes it impossible to separate out the influence of genes from environment.

- The research design is logical. In theory it allows us to see the relative importance of 'nature' (the genes inherited from biological parents) versus 'nurture' (the adoptive family environment).

- Findings of adoption studies give some support to genetic explanations. They show adoptees were more likely to have criminal records if their biological parents had criminal records.

Limitations

- Gottfredson and Hirschi argue that adoption studies show genes have little effect on criminality.

- Adopted children are often placed in environments similar to those of their birth family, with families of the same class and ethnicity, in the same locality etc. Similar environments may produce similar behaviour.

- Many children are not adopted immediately after birth but remain with their biological family for some time. This early environment may be the true cause of their criminality.

> **Question**
> Why might high concordance rates between identical twins not be the result of genetic factors? What other explanation could there be?

Genetic theories (3) XYY syndrome

Key idea Some males have an extra male Y chromosome, which may cause violent behaviour.

Strengths

- Jacob et al found an association between XYY syndrome and offenders imprisoned for violent behaviour.

- Price and Whatmore found some links between the syndrome and property crime.

Limitations

- Even if some violent offenders have the syndrome, this doesn't prove it is the cause of their violence.

- XYY males are tall and well built, so they fit the stereotype of 'violent offenders' and get labelled as such by the courts, so they are more likely to get a prison sentence. As a result, XYY males are over-represented in samples drawn from prisoners and this overstates the importance of the syndrome as a possible cause of crime.

- Alternatively, XYY males may be over-represented in prison because they often have low intelligence, meaning they are more likely to be caught. Samples drawn from prisoners are therefore skewed.

- The syndrome is very rare (only about 1 in 1,000 men have it), so it cannot explain much crime.

Brain injuries and disorders

Key idea Injuries, disorders and diseases of the brain may cause it to malfunction in ways that change personality, morals or self-control, leading to criminal behaviour.

Strengths

- In a few extreme cases, brain injury or disease has led to major changes in an individual's personality and behaviour, including criminality.

- There is some correlation between abnormal EEG readings (which measure brainwave activity) and psychopathic criminality.

- Prisoners are more likely than non-prisoners to have a brain injury.

Limitations

- Crimes caused by brain injury or disease are rare. The sufferer's original personality is more important in whether they engage in crime.

- It is not clear that abnormal brainwave activity causes psychopathic criminality. Some psychopaths have normal EEG patterns and some normal people have abnormal EEG patterns.

- Prisoners' higher likelihood of brain injury could be a result of their criminality (e.g. getting into fights), rather than a cause of it.

Biochemical explanations

Key idea Biochemical factors may trigger criminal behaviour by affecting brain chemistry and mental processes.

Strengths

- Sexual hormones, blood sugar levels and substance abuse can affect mood, judgment and aggression.

- Testosterone levels and male offending both peak around the same age, suggesting hormones affect criminal behaviour.

- Alcohol produces disinhibition, reducing self-control and leading to criminal behaviour, particularly violence. Crack cocaine has been strongly linked to violent crime.

- Biochemical factors are recognised by the courts. The law of infanticide states that if a mother kills her baby as a result of post-natal depression or breastfeeding, she has a partial defence to murder. Pre-menstrual tension (PMT) has been accepted as a defence in shoplifting cases.

Limitations

- Biochemical processes may predispose some individuals to offend, but it may require an environmental 'trigger' to cause actual offending.

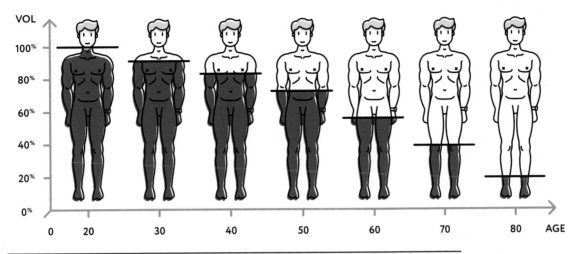

Men's testosterone level declines with age – but much more slowly than their offending.

- Scarmella and Brown found testosterone levels do not greatly affect aggression levels in most men.
- Schalling found high testosterone levels in young males led to verbal aggression, but not physical violence.
- Infanticide may be due to isolation and the responsibility for caring for a newborn child rather than hormones.

General criticisms of biological theories

Environmental factors Biological theories ignore environmental factors. A person's biology may give them *potentially* criminal characteristics (e.g. aggressiveness) but they may need an environmental trigger to engage in a criminal act.

Sample bias Researchers often use studies of convicted criminals, but these may not be representative of the criminals who got away, so they are not a sound basis for generalising about all criminals.

Gender bias Most biological research focuses on males, so it doesn't explain female criminality.

Crime is a social construct. What counts as crime varies between cultures and over time, so it makes no sense to look for universal explanations, as biological theories do.

Evaluating individualistic theories

We can group individualistic theories into four main types: psychodynamic theories; Eysenck's personality theory; learning theories; and cognitive theories. We shall now evaluate these theories, so you might want to have a quick look back at Topic 2.2 to refresh your memory.

Psychodynamic theories (1) Freud

Key idea Freud's psychoanalytic theory explains criminal behaviour in terms of faulty early socialisation preventing the individual resolving unconscious conflicts between the id and the superego.

Strengths

- The theory points to the importance of early socialisation and family relationships in understanding criminal behaviour.
- Psychoanalytic explanations have had some influence on policies for dealing with crime and deviance.

Limitations

- Critics doubt the existence of an 'unconscious mind' – how could we know about it, if it's unconscious?

- Psychoanalytic explanations are unscientific and subjective – they rely on accepting the psychoanalyst's claims that they can see into the workings of the individual's unconscious mind to discover their inner conflicts and motivations.

Psychodynamic theories (2) Bowlby

Key idea Bowlby stresses the importance of the parent-child bond. He sees maternal deprivation as a cause of criminality.

Strengths

- Bowlby's research showed that more of his sample of 44 juvenile delinquents had suffered maternal deprivation (39%) than a control group of non-delinquents (5%).

- His work shows the need to consider the role of parent-child relationships in explaining criminality.

Limitations

- It was a retrospective study, where delinquents and their mothers had to accurately recall past events. This can be a problem, especially if it involves recalling emotive experiences.

- Bowlby accounts for the delinquency of 39% of the children in terms of maternal deprivation but doesn't explain why the other 61% were delinquent. Deprivation cannot be the only cause.

- Bowlby's own later study of 60 children who had been separated from their parents for long periods before they were 5, found no evidence of 'affectionless psychopathy'.

- Bowlby overestimates how far early childhood experiences have a permanent effect on later behaviour. (This is also a criticism of Freud.)

- Sammons and Putwain note that the idea of a link between maternal deprivation and criminality is no longer widely accepted.

Eysenck's personality theory

Key idea Eysenck sees criminality as the result of an extraverted-neurotic (high E, high N) personality. Extraverts seek stimulation, leading to rule-breaking, while neurotics' anxiety prevents them learning from punishment. Psychotic (high P) personalities are also more likely to offend.

Strengths

- The theory is useful in describing how some measurable tendencies could increase a person's risk of offending.

- Eysenck predicts that high E, N and P scores lead to criminality and some studies support his predictions: offenders tend towards being extravert, neurotic and psychotic.

Limitations

- Farrington examined a range of studies. These show prisoners are neurotic and psychotic, but not extraverted.

- The E scale (extraversion) may be measuring two separate things: impulsiveness and sociability. Offenders score highly on impulsiveness (they lack self-control), but not sociability (they are loners).

- Evidence on prisoners shows a correlation between personality type and criminality, but this doesn't prove that personality type *causes* criminality. It could be the other way round: being in prison might cause people to become neurotic.

- Convicted offenders (on whom the theory is based) may not be typical of offenders as a whole. For example, less impulsive (low N) offenders may be more likely to avoid getting caught.

- Eysenck used self-report questionnaires, which may not produce valid results: people may lie when asked about themselves.

> **Question**
>
> From Eysenck's theory, we might expect extraverts to be more likely to commit certain kinds of crime. If so, which kinds and why?

Learning theories (1) differential association

Key idea Sutherland argues that we learn criminal behaviour through socialisation in social groups where the attitudes and values we are exposed to in these groups favour law-breaking.

Strengths

- The fact that crime often runs in families supports the theory. People with criminal parents are more likely to become criminals themselves, perhaps because they have learned criminal values and techniques in the family.
- Matthews found that juvenile delinquents are more likely to have friends who commit anti-social acts, suggesting that they learn their behaviour from peer groups.
- The attitudes of work groups can normalise white collar crime, enabling offenders to justify their behaviour.

Limitations

- Not everyone who is exposed to 'criminal influences' becomes criminal. They might learn from family or peers *how* to commit crime, but never put this into practice.

Learning theories (2) operant learning

Key idea Operant learning theory, or behaviourism, states that if a particular behaviour (including criminal behaviour) results in a desirable outcome (reinforcement), it is likely to be repeated. If it results in an undesirable outcome (punishment), it is unlikely to be repeated.

Strengths

- Skinner's studies of learning in animals show that they learn from experience through reinforcement. Some human learning is also of this kind.
- This can be applied to offending. Jeffery states that if crime leads to more rewarding than punishing outcomes for an individual, they will be more likely to offend.

Limitations

- Operant learning theory is based on studies of learning in animals. This is not an adequate model of how humans learn criminal behaviour.
- The theory ignores internal mental processes such as thinking, personal values and attitudes. It explains criminal behaviour solely in terms of external rewards and punishments.
- Humans have free will and can choose their course of action. For example, we can choose to do something that causes us suffering in order to help someone else.

Skinner studied learning in rats. Do humans learn in the same way?

Learning theories (3) social learning theory

Key idea Bandura argues that we learn behaviour through observation and imitation of others. If we see a model being rewarded for acting in a deviant way, we don't need to experience the reward ourselves in order to copy it.

Strengths

- Unlike Skinner, Bandura takes account of the fact that we are social beings. We learn from the experiences of others, not just from our own direct experience.
- Bandura shows that children who observed aggressive behaviour being rewarded, imitated that behaviour. This shows the importance of role models in learning deviant behaviour.

Limitations

- The theory is based on laboratory studies. Laboratories are artificial settings and findings may not be valid for real-life situations.
- The theory assumes people's behaviour is completely determined by their learning experiences and ignores their freedom of choice. This also conflicts with legal views of crime, which assume that we have free will to commit crime.
- Not all observed behaviour is easily imitated. We might see a film in which a safecracker is rewarded with the 'loot', but we lack the skills to imitate the behaviour.

> ### Question
> What kinds of characteristics do you think a model would need to have, in order for adolescents to imitate the model's behaviour?

Cognitive theories (1) criminal personality theory

Key idea Yochelson and Samenow's theory sees criminal behaviour as the result of errors and biases in criminals' thinking patterns.

Strengths

- The idea that criminals' thinking patterns are different from normal has led to other research. For example, PICTS (the Psychological Inventory of Criminal Thinking Styles) is a questionnaire aimed at revealing whether someone shows criminal thought patterns.
- Successful treatments, known as cognitive behavioural therapy, have been developed based on the idea that criminals' thought processes can be corrected with treatment.

Limitations

- Yochelson and Samenow did not use a control group of non-criminals to see if 'normal' people also make the same thinking errors.
- Their sample was unrepresentative: there were no women and most of the men had been found insane and sent to psychiatric hospital. Yet Yochelson and Samenow claim that *all* offenders share the same thinking errors as this sample.
- There was high sample attrition (drop-out rate). By the end only 30 were left in the study.

Cognitive theories (2) moral development theory

Key idea The theory argues that criminals are stuck at an immature stage of moral development unable to make correct moral choices, which leads to criminal behaviour.

Strengths

- Some studies show delinquents are more likely to have immature moral development, as the theory predicts.

- Thornton and Reid found the theory to be truer for crimes such as theft and robbery (which may involve reasoning) than crimes of violence (which are often impulsive).

Limitations

- Kohlberg focuses on moral *thinking* rather than moral *behaviour*. Someone may be perfectly capable of thinking morally while acting immorally.

ACTIVITY / **Discussion**

Evaluating cognitive theories   Go to www.criminology.uk.net

General criticisms of individualistic theories

Artificiality Researchers often use laboratory experiments, but how someone behaves in a laboratory may not reflect how they would act in reality.

Sample bias Researchers often use studies of convicted criminals, but these may not be representative of the criminals who got away, so they are not a sound basis for generalising about all criminals.

Neglect of social factors They take little account of the social factors that may cause criminal behaviour, such as poverty and discrimination.

Evaluating sociological theories

We can group sociological theories into five types: functionalist and subcultural theories; interactionism and labelling theory; Marxism; left and right realism; and surveillance theories. We shall now evaluate these theories, so you might want to have a quick look back at Topic 2.3 to refresh your memory.

Functionalist and subcultural theories

Functionalism (1) Durkheim

Key idea Society is bound together by shared norms and values, but some rule-breaking is inevitable because not all individuals are adequately socialised.

Strengths

- Durkheim was the first to recognise that crime can have positive functions for society, e.g. reinforcing boundaries between right and wrong by uniting people against the wrongdoer.

Limitations

- Durkheim claims society requires a certain amount of deviance to function but offers no way of knowing how much is the right amount.
- While crime might be functional for some, it is not functional for victims.

Functionalism (2) Merton

Key idea Blocked opportunities to achieve society's goals by legitimate means causes individuals to use criminal means.

Strengths

- Merton shows how both normal and deviant behaviour arise from the same goals. Conformists and innovators both pursue 'money success', but by different means.

- He explains the patterns shown in official statistics: most crime is property crime, because society values wealth so highly; working-class crime rates are higher, because they have less opportunity to obtain wealth legitimately.

Limitations

- Merton ignores crimes of the wealthy and over-predicts the amount of working-class crime.
- He sees deviance solely as an individual response, ignoring the group deviance of delinquent subcultures.
- Merton focuses on utilitarian crime, e.g. theft, ignoring crimes with no economic motive, e.g. vandalism.

Subcultural theories

Key idea Individuals whose legitimate opportunities are blocked may turn to deviant subcultures as an alternative means of achieving status.

Strengths

- These theories show how subcultures perform a function for their members by offering solutions to the problem of failing to achieve mainstream goals legitimately.
- Cloward and Ohlin show how different types of neighbourhood give rise to different *illegitimate* opportunities and different subcultures (criminal, conflict and retreatist).

Limitations

- Like Merton, they ignore crimes of the wealthy and over-predict the amount of working-class crime.
- They assume everyone starts with mainstream goals and turns to a subculture when they fail to achieve them. But some people don't share those goals in the first place; they may be attracted to crime for other reasons.
- Actual subcultures are not as clear-cut as Cloward and Ohlin claim. Some show characteristics of all three types: criminal, conflict and retreatist.

Questions

1. What do you find most convincing about subcultural explanations of criminality?
2. What kinds of crimes and criminals do these theories fail to explain?

Interactionism and labelling theory

Key idea An act only becomes criminal when labelled as such. To understand crime, we must focus on how certain acts and people get labelled as criminal.

Strengths

- Labelling theory shows that the law is not a fixed set of rules to be taken for granted, but something whose construction we need to explain.
- It shifts the focus onto how the police create crime by applying labels based on their stereotypes ('typifications') of the 'typical criminal'. This selective law enforcement may explain why the working class and minority groups are over-represented in the crime statistics.
- It shows how attempts to control deviance can trigger a deviance amplification spiral (e.g. in a moral panic) and create *more* deviance.

Limitations

- It wrongly implies that once someone is labelled, a deviant career is inevitable. (This is called determinism – as though the outcome is pre-determined.)

- Its emphasis on the negative effects of labelling gives offenders a 'victim' status, ignoring the *real* victims.
- It fails to explain why people commit primary deviance in the first place, *before* they are labelled.
- It doesn't explain where the power to label comes from. It focuses on officials such as the police who *apply* the labels, rather than on the capitalist class who *make* the rules.
- It fails to explain why the labels are applied to certain groups (e.g. the working class) but not to others.

> **Question**
> Suggest reasons why working-class people and members of minority ethnic groups appear more likely to be labelled as criminals.

The Marxist view of crime and law

Key idea Capitalism is criminogenic: it is the root cause of crime. All classes commit crime but selective law enforcement means crime appears to be only a working-class problem.

Strengths

- It shows how poverty and inequality can cause working-class crime, and how capitalism promotes greed and encourages upper-class crime.
- It shows how both law-making and law enforcement are biased against the working class and in favour of the powerful. For example, corporate crime is rarely prosecuted.

Limitations

- It focuses on class and largely ignores the relationship between crime and other inequalities, such as gender and ethnicity.
- It over-predicts the amount of working-class crime: not all poor people turn to crime.
- Not all capitalist societies have high crime rates; e.g. Japan's homicide rate is only about a fifth of the USA's. (However, Marxists point out that capitalist societies with little welfare provision, like the USA, have higher crime rates.)

Right realism

Key idea Right realists base their views on rational choice theory (RCT): criminals are rational actors who weigh up the risks and rewards before deciding whether to commit crimes.

Strengths

- Several studies support RCT. Rettig gave students a scenario of an opportunity to commit a crime. He found that the degree of punishment determined whether they chose to commit the crime.
- Feldman found that people made rational decisions: if the rewards were high and risks low, they said the crime was worth committing.
- Bennett and Wright interviewed convicted burglars. The burglars considered the potential reward, difficulty of breaking in and risk of being caught. Risk was the most important factor influencing their decision to commit the crime.
- Right realism may explain some opportunistic petty crimes such as theft.

Limitations

- Rettig and Feldman's studies were experiments; the results may not apply to real offenders.
- Bennett and Wright studied unsuccessful burglars. We don't know if successful burglars also think in this way.

- Not all crimes are the result of rational decisions. Violent crimes are often impulsive. Offenders under the influence of drugs or alcohol may also be unlikely to calculate the risks and rewards before offending.

Left realism

Key idea Left realists see crime as a real problem. Its main victims are disadvantaged groups. Inequality is the main cause of crime; it encourages relative deprivation.

Strengths

- Left realism draws attention to the importance of poverty, inequality and relative deprivation as the underlying structural causes of crime.
- It draws attention to the reality of street crime and its effects, especially on victims from deprived groups.

Limitations

- Henry and Milovanovic argue that left realism accepts the authorities' definition of crime as just being the street crimes of the poor. It fails to explain white collar and corporate crime and ignores the harms done to the poor by the crimes of the powerful.
- It over-predicts the amount of working-class crime: not everyone who experiences relative deprivation and marginalisation turns to crime.
- Its focus on high-crime inner-city areas gives an unrepresentative view and makes crime appear a greater problem than it is.

> **Question**
> Which explanation of criminality do you find more convincing – right realism or left realism? Give your reasons.

Surveillance theories

Key idea Foucault argues that in today's society, people engage in self-surveillance. We are also under electronic surveillance. Surveillance has become an increasingly important form of crime control.

Strengths

- Foucault's work has stimulated research into surveillance and disciplinary power – especially into the idea of an 'electronic Panopticon' that uses modern technologies to monitor us.
- Researchers have identified other forms of surveillance, including actuarial justice and profiling.

Limitations

- Foucault exaggerates the extent of control. For example, Goffman shows how some inmates of prisons and mental hospitals resist controls.
- Surveillance may not change people's behaviour as Foucault claims. For example, studies show that CCTV may fail to prevent crime because offenders often take no notice of it.

General criticisms of sociological theories

The underlying cause Sociologists disagree about the cause of crime, e.g. functionalism and Marxism see structural factors as the cause, whereas labelling theory sees it as the outcome of interactions between police and suspects.

Over-prediction Sociological theories don't explain why not every individual who is deprived or suffering blocked opportunities commits crime.

Biological and psychological factors Sociological theories neglect the factors that may explain why one individual commits crime while another person in exactly the same social position does not.

ACTIVITY / Media

Evaluating theories of crime

Go to www.criminology.uk.net

NOW TEST YOURSELF

Practice Question

What are the strengths and limitations of biological theories in trying to explain the causes of criminality? Read the answer by Yasmin and then answer the questions below.

Answer by Yasmin

The basic idea behind all biological theories is that criminals are biologically different and this causes their criminality. Lombroso's physiological theory measured criminals' physical characteristics (noses, arms etc.), claiming to find they had distinctive features. While this is a scientific approach, he didn't measure a control group of non-criminals.

Sheldon's theory of somatotypes argues that criminals have an innately muscular, mesomorphic body type. However, this may be due to environmental factors such as manual labour, or even labelling.

Genetic theories claim criminals have different genes. They use twin studies and adoption studies to test their effect. Identical twins have the same genes, so if genes cause criminality, then if one twin is criminal, the other will be too – a 100% concordance rate. While studies show higher concordance for identical twins, this is nearer to 50%. Also, identical twins often share identical environments as well as identical genes.

Adoption studies compare adoptees' criminality with their biological and their adoptive parents. A biological parent shares genes with the child, so if they both have criminal records but the adoptive parent does not, genes may be the cause. Studies give some support to this, but adoptees are often placed in families similar to their birth families and this similar environment may cause their criminality.

Biochemical factors may also cause crime. There is good evidence linking alcohol to violent crime, while male offending rates peak around the same age as their testosterone level. However, while both alcohol and testosterone may predispose someone to crime, they may need an environmental 'trigger' to cause actual offending.

Overall, biological theories offer useful insights but are not enough on their own to explain criminality.

Questions

Answer the following questions. Refer back to what you have read in this Topic where necessary.

1. How would using 'a control group of non-criminals' help if you were testing Lombroso's theory?
2. How might labelling account for the fact that mesomorphs appear to commit more crime?
3. What does the 'concordance rate' measure in twin studies?
4. Adoption studies may not necessarily prove that genetic factors are the cause of criminality. What alternative explanation does Yasmin give?
5. What environmental 'triggers' do you think Yasmin is referring to in relation to alcohol and offending?
6. Which biological explanations of criminality does Yasmin cover in her answer? Has she left any out?

Assess the use of criminological theories in informing policy development

Getting started

Working in a small group

1. Choose a theory or group of theories that you have studied.
2. Based on the ideas of your chosen theory, suggest some ways of preventing crime.

Crime control: the influence of theories

Many of the theories that we have studied so far have had an influence on policies to control crime. In this Topic, we look at some of the ways in which biological, individualistic and sociological theories about criminality have influenced or shaped different crime control policies.

Biological theories influencing policies

Biological theories argue that criminality is caused by some physical abnormality within the individual. These theories have led to crime control and punishment policies that aim to change the working of the criminal's brain or body and cure the condition that causes their criminality.

Biochemical processes

Several biochemical processes and factors have been linked with criminality, such as the effects of the male sex hormone testosterone, substance abuse and deficiencies in diet. This has led to policies, mostly in the form of individualised treatment programmes for offenders.

Crime control policies

Treatment programmes to reduce offending include the use of drugs, diet and surgery.

Drug treatments are used in some situations to treat or control criminal or anti-social behaviour. They do this by affecting the body's biochemical processes.

- **Alcohol abuse** can trigger violent behaviour. The drug Antabuse is used in aversion therapy to treat alcoholism. It works by preventing the body from breaking down alcohol, immediately causing very unpleasant 'hangover' symptoms if the user consumes even a small quantity.

- **Heroin addiction** often leads addicts to commit crime to pay for the drug. Methadone is used to treat addicts, as a long-term alternative to heroin or to prevent withdrawal symptoms. By providing a legal, medically controlled substitute, Methadone helps to reduce crime.

- **Sex offenders** Stilbestrol is a form of 'chemical castration' that has been used in prison to treat male sex offenders. Stilbestrol is a female hormone that suppresses testosterone as a way of reducing men's sex drive. However, it can have serious side effects, including breast development, feminisation and serious psychiatric disorders.

- **Managing prisoners** Sedatives and tranquillisers such as Valium, Librium and Largactil have been often used to keep potentially troublesome or violent prisoners calm.

ACTIVITY / Media

Treating drug addiction   Go to www.criminology.uk.net

Diet can be modified to try to change anti-social behaviour.

- Gesch et al found that supplementing prisoners' diets with vitamins, minerals and fatty acids caused a 'remarkable' reduction in anti-social behaviour (of up to 37% in the case of violent incidents).
- Vitamin B3 has been used to treat some forms of schizophrenia, a disorder sometimes associated with violent behaviour.
- Dietary changes have been used to try to control hyperactivity (which may lead to offending) – for example, removing foodstuffs containing the artificial colouring tartrazine from children's diets.

Surgery has been used to alter offender's brains or bodies with the aim of preventing them from offending. This has included the following:

- **Surgical castration** of sex offenders has been used in the past in the attempt to change offending behaviour, for example in Denmark and the USA. However, results have been mixed.
- **Lobotomy** is a major procedure that involves cutting the connection between the frontal lobes of the brain and the thalamus. It has been used to treat paranoid schizophrenia and sexually motivated and spontaneously violent criminals. However, it can have serious side effects and very few lobotomies are now performed.

Crowd control and public order offences In addition to the above individualised treatments, other policies use methods aimed at controlling groups by using chemical substances. For example, tear gas may be used to control crowds or disperse rioters. It works by causing uncomfortable or distressing sensations, including vomiting, breathing difficulties and disorientation. It can also cause lung damage and even death.

Genetic theories: eugenics

Genetic theories of criminality have argued that the tendency to criminality is transmitted by inheriting a 'criminal gene'. The idea that we can identify such a gene is now discredited but in the early 20th century it was associated with a movement known as eugenics.

Eugenicists were obsessed with the fear that the human race was in danger of 'degenerating' because the poor were breeding at a faster rate than the higher classes. As a result, they were passing on supposedly inferior genes for low intelligence, insanity, poverty and criminality more quickly than the higher classes were passing on their 'superior' genes, thus lowering the average intelligence and moral quality of the population.

Compulsory sterilisation

Eugenicists argued that the 'genetically unfit' should therefore be prevented from breeding. This led them to favour policies such as the compulsory sterilisation of 'defectives' such as criminals (since they believed criminality to be hereditary) and those with mental illnesses or learning difficulties.

Eugenicists set up pressure groups to campaign for their policies, which were introduced in several countries. For example, in 1927 the US Supreme Court ruled that it was legal to compulsorily sterilise the 'unfit', including those with learning difficulties, 'for the protection and health of the state'. Other eugenic policies have included forced abortions and restrictions on the right to marry.

The Nazis' 'racial purity' policies

The most extreme case of eugenic policies was that of Nazi Germany (1933-45). The Nazis strongly favoured such policies as a means of 'purifying' the 'Aryan master race' by eliminating those they deemed unfit to breed. Initially they targeted the physically and mentally disabled, with 400,000 people sterilised against their will and 70,000 killed under the Nazis' euthanasia policy.

The Holocaust Ultimately, eugenic policies became part of the justification for the Nazis' genocide of supposedly 'inferior' races during the Second World War. These included Jews, of whom at least 6 million were killed, and Gypsies/Roma, of whom up to 1.5 million were murdered. In addition, many thousands of others defined as 'deviants' were killed, including gays and lesbians, drug users, alcoholics and the homeless.

ACTIVITY / Discussion

The ethics of biological policies   Go to www.criminology.uk.net

Individualistic theories influencing policies

Individualistic theories of offending have been used to develop treatment programmes aimed at reducing offending behaviour. Here we shall examine a range of these programmes.

Psychoanalysis

Psychoanalysis is based on Freud's theory of personality. This highlights the unconscious conflicts between the id (instincts) and the superego (conscience). Psychoanalysis sees a weak superego as a cause of criminality, since the individual lacks a moral force to curb their selfish instincts. A weak superego can result from inadequate early socialisation of the child.

Crime control

Treatment is very lengthy (Freud saw his patients five times a week, often for years). It involves bringing these unconscious conflicts and repressed emotions into the conscious mind so they can be resolved. To access the unconscious mind, Freud used hypnosis and free association, where the analyst gives the patient a word and they respond with the first word that comes into their mind.

Aichhorn applied psychoanalytic ideas to policies for treating young offenders at the institution he supervised. Because they had uncaring or absent parents, they had failed to develop loving relationships. Normal socialisation had not taken place and so they had not developed a superego. This is similar to Bowlby's idea that maternal deprivation can cause criminality.

Aichhorn rejected the harsh environments of young offenders' institutions at the time (the 1920s) and treated the children by providing a happy and pleasant environment that would make development of the superego possible.

ACTIVITY / Media

Psychoanalysis   Go to www.criminology.uk.net

Is it effective?

Psychoanalysis does not seem very effective. Eysenck found that only 44% of psychoanalysis patients treated for neurosis showed improvement, as against 72% of patients treated by hospitals or GPs. If psychoanalysis doesn't work for neurosis, it seems unlikely to work for criminals (who Eysenck argues are likely to be neurotics).

Cost Psychoanalysis is costly and time-consuming, so it has never been used on a large scale for treating criminals.

Abuse Psychoanalysis gives analysts the power to define what is normal or abnormal. For example, Freud regarded homosexuality as abnormal. Imposing their definitions in this way can give rise to abuse.

Operant learning and token economies

Operant learning theory (also called behaviourism) states that criminal behaviour is learned through reinforcement and punishment. It has been applied to policies for offenders via token economies. A token economy is a behaviour modification programme used in some prisons.

Crime control

A token economy works in this way:

- The institution draws up a list of desirable behaviours, e.g. obeying the rules, interacting positively with staff.
- When the offender behaves in the desired way, they earn a token.
- Tokens may be exchanged for rewards, e.g. sweets, phone calls.
- Through this selective reinforcement, good behaviour becomes more likely and undesirable behaviour less likely.

Is it effective?

Some studies show an improvement in behaviour, but once the reinforcement stops (when the offender leaves prison), the behaviours tend to disappear. However, offenders return to crime more slowly compared with those who have not undergone the programme. Token economies also make prisoners more manageable while in prison.

There have been cases in the USA of food or drink being withheld and used as 'rewards'. Critics argue that these are a human right, not a privilege to be earned.

Aversion therapy and Eysenck's theory

Aversion therapy applies Eysenck's personality theory to the treatment of sex offenders. Eysenck states that criminals tend to be strongly extravert and neurotic. This makes them harder to condition because they are more resistant to learning through punishment.

Conditioning therefore needs to be 'stronger' in order to change the sex offender's behaviour, as follows:

- Offenders are asked to think about an unacceptable sexual fantasy until they are aroused.
- A strongly aversive stimulus (one the individual would choose to avoid) is then administered, such as an electric shock or a nausea-inducing drug.
- The procedure is repeated until the offender comes to associate the deviant arousal and the stimulus. The aim is to stop the thoughts and thus stop the offending behaviour.

Is it effective?

Aversion therapy has had very limited success, usually only short term, and its use in attempting to 'cure' gay people has also been criticised as a human rights abuse.

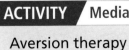

ACTIVITY / **Media**

Aversion therapy

Go to www.criminology.uk.net

Cognitive theories and CBT

Cognitive theories have been applied to a range of offender treatment programmes known as cognitive behavioural therapy (CBT).

Cognitive theories state that our cognitions (thought processes) shape our behaviour, including offending behaviour. Offenders have 'distorted cognitions' that lead them to offend. CBT programmes aim to change offenders' thoughts and attitudes so as to change their behaviour. Below are two examples of CBT programmes in the UK.

One-to-one therapy session addressing anger management issues.

Think First

Think First is a programme of group and one-to–one sessions for repeat offenders on probation. It aims to enable offenders to control their thoughts, feelings and behaviour. It teaches problem-solving skills, consequential thinking (what will be consequences of my course of action, for me and others?), decision making and seeing things from the other's point of view (perspective taking). It also provides social interaction and moral reasoning training.

Is it effective? Those completing the programme are 30% less likely to be re-convicted than offenders who receive an alternative community sentence. However, the non-completion rate is often high.

Aggression Replacement Training (ART)

ART is a programme for violent or aggressive offenders. It involves:

- Interpersonal skills training, e.g. through role play.
- Anger control techniques, dealing with emotions and providing offenders with alternative courses of action instead of violence.
- Moral reasoning training that challenges their attitudes by confronting them with moral dilemmas to consider.

Is it effective? Evaluations mostly show lower re-conviction rates. However, some evaluations have found that although thinking skills improved, behaviour did not.

ACTIVITY / Media

Cognitive behavioural therapy   Go to www.criminology.uk.net

'What works'

Not all CBT programmes are equally successful or equally suitable. For example, there would be little point putting a non-violent burglar on an ART programme.

The Home Office's 'what works' policy aims to ensure that CBT programmes actually reduce offending and so it only accredits ones that meet certain criteria:

- A clear plan and proven methods for altering offenders' behaviour.
- Careful matching of offenders to the right programme, in terms of their offence, risk of re-offending and learning abilities (e.g. illiterate offenders may need a different programme from literate ones)
- Targeting the risk factors that lead to offending.

A successful programme must show that it improves offenders' skills and their everyday behaviour and reduces their re-offending.

Sociological theories influencing policies

Sociological theories of offending have been used to propose several policies aimed at crime control.

Merton and subcultural theories

For Merton, in America (and to a large extent the UK), the main social goal is to gain wealth. However, the poor find their opportunity to do so legitimately (e.g. through a good education) is blocked. Many adapt to this by 'innovating' – using illegal means such as theft.

Subcultural theorists (such as Albert Cohen, and Cloward and Ohlin) also argue that crime is caused by blocked opportunities. Different subcultures cope with this by becoming professional criminals, joining gangs or dropping out.

Crime control and punishment policies

Merton's strain theory provides a basis for crime control and reduction policies. Society's structure could be made more equal in these ways:

- **Policies to tackle poverty**, Better welfare benefits, wages and job security would reduce crime by giving everyone a more equal chance of achieving success by legal means.
- **Equal opportunities in school** Treating working-class pupils equally would reduce their failure rate, making them less likely to suffer status frustration and join delinquent subcultures.
- **Education in prison** Half of UK prisoners have a reading age of 11. Better education in prisons would help inmates gain skills to get a good job and go straight.

Are these policies effective?

Evidence shows that anti-poverty policies have a positive effect. Societies that spend more on welfare jail fewer people. Those with greater inequality, like the USA, have higher crime rates.

ACTIVITY / Research

Improving benefits   Go to www.criminology.uk.net

Labelling theory

Labelling theory argues that much crime is the result of a self-fulfilling prophecy. By labelling someone as criminal, we risk them living up to their label and committing further, more serious crimes. Labelling theory has influenced the development of several crime control policies.

Decriminalisation

Decriminalising minor offences such as possession of cannabis would mean many fewer young people were labelled as criminals. A criminal record can prevent them getting a job and lead to secondary deviance (further offending).

Diversion policies

These aim to keep an offender out of the justice system so as to avoid labelling them as criminals. Some diversion policies are informal, like when police use their discretion not to charge someone. Others are formal, such as requiring an offender to attend an anger management programme to avoid prosecution.

Reintegrative shaming

Braithwaite identifies two types of 'shaming' or labelling:

- **Disintegrative shaming**, where both the crime and the criminal are labelled as bad and the offender is excluded from society. This can push them into secondary deviance.
- **Reintegrative shaming** labels the act but not the actor – as if to say, 'he has done a bad thing', rather than 'he is a bad person'. It avoids stigmatising the offender as evil, while still encouraging them to repent and encouraging others to admit them back into society.

Are these policies effective?

Evidence shows crime control policies based on labelling theory can deal successfully with minor offences and young offenders. By avoiding labelling people as criminals and keeping them out of the justice system, they avoid pushing individuals into a deviant career.

Right realism

Right realists see criminals as making a rational choice to commit crime. Their view has led to three main crime control and punishment policies.

1 Situational crime prevention (SCP)

SCP policies aim to reduce the opportunities for crime by increasing the risks or difficulties of committing the crime and by reducing the rewards. SCP is based on rational choice theory: the idea that offenders act rationally, weighing up the risks and rewards of a crime opportunity.

SCP includes 'target hardening' measures, such as locking cars, employing security guards and re-shaping the environment to 'design crime out' of an area.

Target hardening, Westminster Bridge, following a terrorist attack when a car mounted the pavement, killing six.

Is SCP effective?

One problem is displacement. If criminals are rational actors, then when they find a target too hard to crack, they will simply look for a softer one. For example, they may commit crime at a different time or place, use a different method or choose a different target (victim). This may result in more vulnerable targets (such as the old, poor or disabled) being victimised more because other targets have been hardened.

2 Environmental crime prevention

Wilson and Kelling's 'broken windows' theory argues that a disorderly neighbourhood sends out the message that nobody cares. This attracts offenders, who calculate that their activities there will not be investigated. Serious crime will increase and law-abiding citizens will move out if they can.

Wilson and Kelling argue for a twofold policy:

- **An environmental improvement strategy** All signs of disorder must be tackled promptly – graffiti removed, broken windows repaired etc.
- **A zero tolerance policing (ZTP) strategy** – taking a tough, 'zero tolerance' stance towards all crime, even the most trivial. Police should concentrate on tackling 'quality of life' offences, such as aggressive begging, prostitution and vandalism.

Is ZTP effective?

- Crime fell after ZTP was introduced in New York in the 1990s, but this may have been due to other factors: US cities that had *not* adopted ZTP also saw crime fall.
- Males and Macallair found that ZTP curfews can *increase* juvenile crime: by removing law-abiding youths from the streets, they leave them emptier and favourable to crime.
- ZTP can lead to targeting of ethnic minorities due to police racism, and to confrontations due to heavy-handed 'military policing'.
- ZTP and SCP fail to tackle structural causes of crime such as inequality. Also, they focus on low-level street crime, ignoring the crimes of the powerful: white collar and state crime.

3 Penal populism and imprisonment

Right realists argue that criminals make a rational choice to offend by weighing up the costs and benefits of offending. Higher costs such as tougher penalties should therefore deter criminals.

'Prison works' From the 1990s governments began to take the view that tougher penalties were needed, arguing that 'prison works'. In the right realist view, prison has two functions:

- **Incapacitation** Criminals become incapable of harming the public – jail takes them 'out of circulation'.
- **Deterrence** Criminals think twice before offending when they see tough punishments handed out.

Politicians believed tough penalties were popular with the public and so this policy came to be known as 'penal populism'. For example, in 1997 the Conservatives brought in the Crime (Sentences) Act, which introduced mandatory minimum sentences for repeat offenders:

- automatic life sentences for a second serious sexual or violent offence
- a minimum of seven years for a third Class A drug trafficking conviction
- a minimum of three years for a third domestic burglary conviction.

Tony Blair's New Labour government came to power in 1997. Promising to be 'tough on crime and tough on the causes of crime', they introduced measures such as ASBOs and curfews.

Penal populism has led to rising numbers in jail, from 45,000 in 1993 to 80,000 by 2021. England and Wales imprison a bigger proportion of their population than any other Western European country. Meanwhile, in 2020, there were 76 suicides, five homicides, 65,000 incidents of self-harm and 9,800 assaults on staff.

A typical jail. How true is it to say that 'prison works'?

Is prison effective?

Incapacitation Prison might be said to 'work' temporarily – offenders can't commit crimes against the public while they are in jail. However, they may offend against fellow inmates and staff.

Rehabilitation One function of prison is to rehabilitate offenders, but overcrowding and budget cuts mean many prisoners lack access to education, skills training or treatment programmes that would help them become law-abiding citizens.

Recidivism Imprisonment is ineffective in preventing recidivism (repeat offending): 48% of adults are re-convicted within a year of release.

Deterrence Right realists argue that the risk of jail deters would-be criminals, who make rational choices about offending. However, studies show that risk of imprisonment doesn't deter offenders enough to affect overall crime rates.

ACTIVITY / Media

Does prison work?   Go to www.criminology.uk.net

Left realism

Left realists see the root cause of crime as an unequal and unfair social structure. Their theory has been applied via three main policies to reduce crime.

1 Policies to reduce inequality

Left realists call for major structural changes to tackle discrimination, inequality of opportunity and unfairness of rewards, and to provide good jobs and housing for all. This would reduce relative deprivation – the main cause of crime.

2 Democratic policing

The police are losing public support, especially in poorer areas, where they are widely distrusted. Their flow of information dries up and they have to rely on 'military policing', such as stop and searches. This creates further loss of cooperation, meaning they cannot tackle crime effectively.

To win back public support, the police must involve local communities in deciding their priorities. They must focus on crimes that victimise the disadvantaged, such as domestic violence and hate crimes, rather than offences such as possession of soft drugs.

There has been some success for left realist policing policies:

- Neighbourhood policing and police community support officers (PCSOs) have been introduced to build better relationships with communities.
- Many forces now make cannabis possession a low priority crime.
- Domestic violence and hate crime are now a higher priority.

3 A multi-agency approach

Left realists argue that crime control must involve many other agencies apart from the police: schools, youth services, housing departments, social services, the probation service and NHS. Local councils can improve facilities for young people to provide alternatives to crime.

No Knives, Better Lives is an example of a multi-agency, 'joined up' approach aimed at reducing knife crime. This involves a wide range of agencies, including schools, local councils' leisure and youth services, and voluntary organisations as well as the police.

New Labour policies

Some of the policies advocated by left realists reflect the approach of the New Labour governments from 1997 to 2010, which aimed to be 'tough on crime, tough on the causes of crime'. For example, Labour invested in improvements to deprived neighbourhoods through the 'Communities that Care' programme – an example of being tough on the causes of crime.

ACTIVITY / Research

Left and right realism   Go to www.criminology.uk.net

Surveillance theories

Surveillance theories have influenced two major crime control policies: CCTV and profiling.

CCTV

CCTV is a modern form of the Panopticon: a surveillance system in which prison guards can observe inmates without the prisoners knowing whether they were being watched. Foucault argues that this leads prisoners to monitor and regulate their own behaviour.

Is CCTV effective?

Like the Panopticon, CCTV depends on criminals believing they are being watched and being deterred by this. Gill and Loveday found that very few criminals were put off by CCTV. Norris found CCTV has little effect other than displacement.

CCTV has had some successes, such as the identification of David Copeland, a right-wing terrorist convicted of a nail-bombing campaign. However, cameras rarely catch someone 'in the act'. Critics suggest that CCTV's real function may be to reassure the public, even though it makes little difference to their security.

Stereotyping Norris and Armstrong found CCTV operators using racist stereotypes, singling out Black youths for surveillance.

'Surveillance creep' is where technology introduced for one purpose gets extended to another. The introduction of automatic number-plate recognition (ANPR) cameras in the City of London in response to an IRA bombing campaign in 1990-93 failed to identify a single bomber. Instead, the cameras were just used to identify untaxed vehicles. Critics argue that this was a disproportionate use of highly intrusive technology.

ACTIVITY / Research

The surveillance debate   Go to www.criminology.uk.net

Profiling

Profiling involves using data to draw up a statistical picture of likely offenders, often using official crime statistics to do so. Individuals can be profiled according to specific characteristics to decide what degree of risk they pose.

For example, airport security screening checks are based on offender 'risk factors'. Using information gathered about passengers (e.g. their age, sex or nationality), they can be given a risk score (e.g. young males may score higher than old females). Anyone scoring above a given level can be stopped, questioned and searched etc.

Is profiling effective?

Profiling can be discriminatory. A profile based on official crime statistics may show certain groups as more likely to offend, e.g. Black youths. This can create a self-fulfilling prophecy:

- The police act on the profile by stopping Black youths more than other groups.
- Any Black youths who are actually offending are more likely to be caught than offenders from other groups.
- Black youths thus continue to be over-represented in the statistics and this will seem to confirm the profile. The police will continue to target Black youths – a vicious circle.

NEW TEST YOURSELF

Practice Question

With reference to **two** examples, assess how sociological theories of criminality have informed policy development.

(9 marks)

Source: WJEC Criminology Unit 2 examination 2020

Advice

Choose two policies from Topic 4.1 and assess how sociological theories have influenced them.

One way to tackle this is to choose policies that reflect a particular theory. For example, situational crime prevention (SCP), zero tolerance policing, and penal populism/imprisonment all reflect right realist ideas. Start by describing the theory's key ideas (e.g. for right realism, that criminals make a rational choice to offend based on calculating risk versus reward).

Then describe the first policy, explaining how it reflects right realist ideas. E.g., SCP uses target hardening to deter criminals by raising the risks or costs. Next, assess how effective it is; e.g. target hardening may just lead to displacement of crime onto more vulnerable victims.

Repeat these steps for your second policy. Remember to use the relevant specialist terms relating to the theory and policies, including naming any specific Acts of Parliament.

Explain how social changes affect policy development

Working with a partner

1. Turn back to Topic 1.2 and look through the section headed 'How laws change over time'. This covers five areas in which laws have changed: homosexuality; drugs; gun control; children; and physical punishment.

2. Make a list of the reasons why these laws changed. Are there any common factors? Could any of these reasons be described as changes in values?

This Topic is about how social changes affect policies and laws. It examines how cultural changes in norms, values and attitudes, the public's perception of crime and demographic (population) changes have affected policies. We use three main examples to illustrate these changes: drink driving, race relations and LGBT rights.

Social values, norms and mores

Social values, norms and mores are all aspects of culture that regulate people's behaviour.

Values

As we saw in Topic 1.1, values are general principles, beliefs or guidelines about how we should live our lives. They tell us what is right and wrong, good and bad. Different societies may have different values.

- For example, modern societies such as the UK place a high value on pursuing individual wealth.
- By contrast, tribal societies place more value on the group than on the individual. Individuals may have a duty to share their wealth with others.

Norms

Norms are specific rules or socially accepted standards about how we are expected to behave in specific situations. These norms can be informal, unwritten rules, such as that you should not queue-jump, or formal, written rules, such as the law that says you must not drive with more than a certain level of alcohol in your blood.

ACTIVITY	Media

Norms

Go to www.criminology.uk.net

Specific norms are often based on general values. For example, modern society values the principle that all individuals are of equal worth. From this value come specific norms making it illegal to discriminate against someone based on their race, sex or sexual orientation.

Mores

Mores (pronounced *mor-rays*) are very basic, essential norms that society sees as vital for maintaining standards of decency and civilised behaviour. In other words, mores are society's most important moral rules.

One example is the taboo against incest (sexual relationships between close relatives) which is found in all societies. Another is the prohibition against taking human life other than in very exceptional circumstances. Going against a society's mores is likely to be severely punished.

Public perception of crime: drink driving

As we saw in Topic 1.2, laws can change over time. Laws often change because of changes in a society's culture – its norms and values. These changes in values can affect the public's perception of crime: an act that used to be acceptable may now be seen as wrong by today's values.

Drink driving is an example of this. Over time, views about drink driving have changed and this has led to changes in laws and policies. The public have come to see it as much more serious and the laws governing it have become tighter.

In 1925, the first law was passed making driving while drunk an offence. However, there was no clear definition of 'drunk' and no legal limit on how much alcohol drivers could have in their blood, so it was left to the police and courts to decide whether someone was fit to drive.

For many years, public attitudes to drink driving were quite tolerant and it was not generally thought of as a serious offence. Governments showed little interest and did not bother even to collect figures on the number of deaths caused by drink driving.

Think before you drink before you drive.

An early poster from the *THINK!* drink driving campaign.

Meanwhile car ownership was increasing. In 1951, only 15% of households owned a car, but by 1971 this had risen to 55%. This resulted in more deaths: from about 5,000 in 1950 to 8,000 by the 1960s.

Changing perceptions

As a result, the public's perception of drink driving began to change. Road safety was becoming more of a public concern and moving up the political agenda. For example, from 1966 all new cars had to be fitted with seat belts.

Due to public concern about accidents caused by drink driving, the 1967 Road Safety Act introduced a blood alcohol limit of 80mg of alcohol per 100ml of blood. It became an offence to be in charge of a motor vehicle with an alcohol level above this limit.

Breathalysers

In 1968, the first breathalysers were introduced for roadside use. Together with a major advertising campaign by the government, this helped to reduce road deaths by over 1,100 and serious injuries by over 11,000. Importantly, the proportion of accidents where alcohol was involved also fell, from 25% to 15%.

Tougher laws

In 1983 the High Risk Offender scheme was introduced for convicted drivers with an alcohol problem. This group includes drivers who have been disqualified more than once for drink driving. They now have to undergo a medical before they can get their licence back.

In 1991 a new offence of causing death by driving while under the influence of alcohol or drugs was introduced, with a compulsory prison sentence of up to five years. (In 2014, this was increased to 14 years.) The penalty for a first drink driving offence is now up to six months' imprisonment, an unlimited fine and a driving ban for at least one year, with heavier penalties for repeat offenders.

The new laws and tougher sentences reflect growing public intolerance of drink driving. As Table 2 shows, deaths from accidents involving alcohol have been falling over the long term, largely due to tighter restrictions on drink driving. Now only about 5% of road casualties involve alcohol.

1979	1,640
1989	840
1999	460
2009	380
2019	240

Table 2 Deaths from drink driving

Campaigns

The first TV advertising campaign against drink driving mounted by the government was aired over 50 years ago and the fall in deaths is partly due to these campaigns. They have sometimes targeted specific groups who are most at risk of drink driving, such as young men.

The campaigns have been an important factor in changing public perceptions of drink driving as a crime. For example, in 1979, half of all male drivers admitted drink driving at least once a week. However, by 2014, a survey by the government's THINK! campaign against drink driving showed there has been a massive change in people's attitudes.

The survey found that 91% of people agreed that drink driving was unacceptable and 92% said they would feel ashamed if they were caught drinking and driving.

However, road safety campaigns such as Brake argue that that government needs to go further. One in eight road deaths still involves a driver over the alcohol limit and England and Wales have the highest legal alcohol limit in Europe. Brake call for it to be lowered to 20mg. Their survey in 2016 found that over half of drivers agreed.

ACTIVITY Media

Campaigns and changing views

Go to www.criminology.uk.net

Demographic changes: immigration and racism

In 1945, there were fewer than 20,000 non-White residents in the UK. The main immigrant groups were both White: the Irish, who had come for economic reasons, and Jews, who had fled from persecution in Europe.

Demographic changes During the 1950s and 1960s, non-White immigrants came from former British colonies in the Caribbean, the Indian subcontinent and Africa. More recently, people have come from Eastern Europe. Mostly these groups came in search of economic opportunities, often filling jobs that the British refused to take.

As a result, the UK's demographic (population) structure has changed to a multi-ethnic one, as Table 3 shows.

Ethnic group	Population (2011 Census)	% of population
White or White British	55,010,359	87.1
Gypsy/Traveller/Irish Traveller	63,193	0.1
Asian or Asian British	4,373,339	6.9
Black or Black British	1,904,684	3.0
Mixed or Multiple	1,250,229	2.0
Other Ethnic Group	580,374	0.9
Total	63,182,178	100

Table 3 The UK's ethnic diversity

The Windrush generation

However, the early arrivals, known as the 'Windrush generation' (after the *Empire Windrush*, the first ship to bring Caribbean migrants to Britain), faced hostility, with many White people holding racist stereotypes of Black people as dirty, diseased or criminal.

Discrimination Throughout the 1950s and 60s, immigrants often met with discrimination in housing, employment and services. In 1956, a survey in Birmingham found that only 1.5% of Whites would be willing to let a room to a Black tenant. A BBC documentary found churches turning away Black families to avoid upsetting White worshippers.

At the time, it was legal to discriminate against a person on grounds of race. This led to exploitation by landlords letting slum housing to immigrants, who frequently could only get low-paid, low-skilled jobs, even when well qualified.

The Race Relations Acts

As a result of widespread racial discrimination, a Race Relations Act was passed in 1965. This banned racial discrimination in public places and made the promotion of hatred on grounds of 'colour, race, or ethnic or national origins' an offence. A further Race Relations Act in 1968 outlawed discrimination in the key areas of employment, housing and public services.

Both Acts were replaced by the 1976 Race Relations Act, which significantly strengthened the law by extending it to cover both direct and indirect discrimination:

- **Direct discrimination** is when someone treats you less favourably, for example because of your colour.

- **Indirect discrimination** is when there is a policy or rule that applies to everyone, but it has a worse effect on some groups than others. For example, a council may rule that to get on the housing waiting list, you must have lived in the area for five years. This applies to everyone, but a recently arrived homeless refugee family would be disadvantaged by the rule.

In 2010, the Race Relations Act was replaced by the Equality Act, which brought together laws on racial, sex, age and disability discrimination. It is overseen by the Equality and Human Rights Commission.

Cultural changes

Since the 1960s, there has been a cultural change – a decline in prejudice towards ethnic minorities. The 1987 British Attitudes Survey found that 39% of people said they were racially prejudiced, whereas by 2017 this had fallen to 26%.

Similarly, according to a 2018 survey by British Future, 66% of the over 65s in ethnic minorities said the level of racial prejudice today is lower than it was in 1968, while both minorities and the wider population are at ease with the idea of mixed-race relationships and a more integrated society.

Public perception of crime As a result of changing attitudes, there has been a change in the public perception of discrimination and race hate as crimes. People are now more likely to accept that these should be criminal offences.

Reasons for the change

This is partly due to changes in the law. According to some psychologists, if we are made to change our behaviour, we tend to change our attitudes to fit. Thus, if the law is changed to forbid discrimination, people may abandon their prejudiced attitudes to bring them into line with how they are now required to behave.

However, other factors may also be responsible for the decline in prejudice. For example, the British Future survey found that people thought children of different backgrounds mixing at school, and workplace contact with people from other ethnicities, were both more important than race relations laws in improving race relations in Britain.

Continuing discrimination

There have clearly been changes in attitudes and behaviour since the demographic changes brought by immigration. However, this does not mean discrimination has disappeared. As well as racism towards non-Whites, there is Islamophobia, racism towards White East Europeans and Gypsies/Roma, and antisemitism towards Jews. In 2018 The Conservative government was accused of creating a 'hostile environment' that led to the wrongful deportation of members of the 'Windrush generation' who had lived in the UK for decades.

1948. The *Empire Windrush* brings 802 migrants from British colonies in the Caribbean.

ACTIVITY / Media

Demographic changes and policy

Go to www.criminology.uk.net

Cultural changes and LGBT rights

Lesbian, gay, bisexual and transgender (LGBT) rights in the UK have changed dramatically in recent times in line with changes in society's culture and values.

Before the 1960s

For centuries, same-sex sexual activity was condemned as immoral or sinful and severely punished by the law. For example, the 1533 Buggery Act made sodomy between men punishable by death and men were executed until as late as 1835.

Although the death penalty for sodomy was abolished in 1861, an Act of 1885 extended the laws to include any kind of sexual activity between men. (Sexual activity between women has never been a crime in the UK.)

In the 20th century, the law continued to be enforced against gay men. By 1954 there were over 1,000 men in prison as a result, and trials of individuals such as the wartime code-breaker Alan Turing, who played a central role in cracking the codes of the Nazis' Enigma cipher machine. (One estimate suggests that Turing's work shortened the Second World War by over two years and saved 14 million lives.) Turing committed suicide in 1954.

Decriminalisation: the 1967 Act

The persecution of such high-profile individuals led to an outcry and a committee was established under Sir John Wolfenden to review the law. His report recommended decriminalisation of sexual activity in private between men aged 21 and over. This became law in 1967 in England and Wales. Organisations such as the Campaign for Homosexual Equality (CHE) played an important part in lobbying for the change.

Changing values and attitudes

Attitudes towards homosexuality have changed considerably in recent decades and today about two-thirds of the population see nothing wrong in same-sex relationships, compared with a fifth or less in the 1980s. More people now take the view that consenting adults should have the right to do as they wish in private and that this is no business of the police or courts.

We can see this change in attitudes in relation to three other cultural changes: individualism, equal rights and secularisation.

Individualism

Individualism is the belief that individuals should have the right to choose how they live their lives, so long as they do no harm to others. Individualism has become a central value in today's culture and can be seen in many areas of life and the law, such as divorce and abortion as well as sexual preferences.

Equal rights

Another major change in British culture has been the growth of the idea of equal rights. This can be seen in the case of the growth of women's rights and equal treatment regardless of race, colour or religion, all of which have been enshrined in equality laws. The move towards equal rights for LGBT people is part of this trend.

Secularisation

This refers to the declining influence of religion on people's lives, attitudes and values. Religions have generally opposed homosexuality, often violently. However, religion today wields much less influence than in the past – less than half of Britons now believe in God. As a result, religious condemnation of homosexuality carries much less weight and in fact, some churches have softened their attitudes, even permitting gay priests.

Further legal changes

As a result of these changes in society's culture and values, there has been continued progress towards ending discrimination and achieving legal equality for all, regardless of sexual orientation. Several key changes to the law have occurred:

- **Equal age of consent** In 1994, the age of consent was lowered from 21 to 18 and in 2000 it was equalised with heterosexual sex at 16.
- **Civil partnerships** for same-sex couples were introduced in 2005, giving legal recognition and protection to same-sex relationships. In 2019 civil partnerships also became available to heterosexual couples as an alternative to marriage.
- **Same-sex marriage** Previously, marriage was legally defined as being between a man and a woman. This changed in England and Wales with the 2013 Marriage (Same Sex Couples) Act.

Transgender rights

For many years, transsexualism was widely regarded as a medical condition, but attitudes and values have changed rapidly in recent years, with widespread (though not universal) acceptance that individuals should have the right to decide their gender.

The 2004 Gender Recognition Act enables people to apply for a gender recognition certificate, which then allows them to change their legal gender, acquire a new birth certificate and have their acquired sex recognised in law for all purposes. To obtain a gender recognition certificate, they must have spent two years transitioning and they must apply to a gender recognition panel with medical evidence of a diagnosis of gender dysphoria.

Since the 2004 Act was passed, campaigners have called for the right to legally self-declare one's gender identity without going before a panel or supplying medical evidence. However, in 2020, the Conservative government decided to reject the idea of self-declaration and individuals must still apply to a panel and supply medical evidence.

Continuing discrimination

Despite legal changes, LGBT people still face discrimination and according to the LGBT campaigning organisation Stonewall, one in five gay people and two in five trans people experience a hate crime or incident because of their sexuality or identity every year.

ACTIVITY / Media

The impact of cultural change on policy

Go to www.criminology.uk.net

NOW TEST YOURSELF

Practice Question

Discuss how social changes can affect policy development. (9 marks)

Source: WJEC Criminology Unit 2 examination 2017

Advice

You need to focus on how or why society has changed and how this has affected policy development.

Take one or more examples such as race relations, homosexuality, drink driving or other areas where social changes have affected policies. Use the terms values, norms and mores in your answer. Describe any policies or laws that have been introduced and explain the social changes that brought about these new laws or policies.

For race relations, describe the 1965, 1968, 1976 and 2010 legislation. Discuss demographic changes caused by immigration, cultural changes such as declining prejudice, acceptance of 'mixed' relationships, the experience of attending school or working with members of other ethnic groups, and willingness to see discrimination and racial hatred as crimes.

For homosexuality, include decriminalisation (1967), age of consent (1994 and 2000), civil partnerships (2004) and same-sex marriage (2014). Use changes such as individualism, equal rights, and secularisation. You could also refer to changes relating to transgender rights.

Discuss how campaigns affect policy making

Getting started

Working with a partner, look back at the campaigns you studied for Unit 1, Topics 2.1 and 2.2.

1. Note any examples of the following types of campaign: newspaper campaigns; individual campaigns; pressure group campaigns.
2. Which of the campaigns were aimed at changing policies and laws?
3. Why might these ways of campaigning be successful?

Share your answers with the rest of the class.

Campaigns often aim to affect policy making, for example changing the law so as to create a new criminal offence. Campaigns may be led by a newspaper, a lone individual or a pressure group. In this Topic we look at some examples of how such campaigns can affect policy making.

Newspaper campaigns to affect policy making

Newspapers can play an important role in policy making, especially through campaigning to change the law. The following two examples show how newspapers can help to shape the law by mobilising public opinion so that government takes action.

Sarah's Law

As we saw in Unit 1, Topic 2.1, the Child Sex Offender Disclosure Scheme, or 'Sarah's Law', was the result of a successful campaign to allow parents, carers and others to ask the police if a convicted sex offender has contact with a specific child. The campaign came about following the abduction and murder in July 2000 of 8-year-old Sarah Payne in West Sussex by Roy Whiting. Whiting had been convicted in 1995 of abducting and indecently assaulting another 8-year-old girl.

The News of the World's role

The campaign for Sarah's Law was championed by the *News of the World* newspaper and backed by Sarah's parents, who had been convinced from the start that a sex offender had murdered their daughter. This was confirmed when Whiting was convicted of the crime in 2001 and it was revealed that he had a previous conviction for a sexual offence against a child.

The newspaper's support was central to the campaign's success. In July 2000, it 'named and shamed' fifty people it claimed were paedophiles. The paper promised to continue until it had revealed the identity of every paedophile in Britain.

Success The campaign eventually succeeded in persuading the government to introduce the Child Sex Offender Disclosure Scheme throughout England and Wales in 2011. However, it should be noted that while anyone can ask the police if someone in contact with a child has a record of child sexual offences, the police are not obliged to disclose information and will only do so if they judge that the child is at risk of harm and the disclosure is necessary to safeguard the child.

The year and a day rule

Michael Gibson was 20 when he was assaulted by David Clark in Darlington town centre in April 1992. Michael died after being in a coma for 22 months. Clark could only be charged with grievous bodily harm and was jailed for two years. He was free before Michael died.

At the time, the 'year and a day' rule existed. It was a law dating back to 1278 . The rule said that if victims of an assault lived for a year and a day, their attackers could not be tried for manslaughter or murder.

The Northern Echo's role

Michael's mother Pat sought to change the law. In her support, the *Northern Echo* newspaper launched the 'Justice for Michael' campaign, urging its readers to sign a petition

The *News of the World* office: collecting signatures for the petition.

demanding that the year and a day rule be scrapped. With Pat Gibson's permission, the *Echo* published a front-page photo of Michael in a coma in his hospital bed. Thousands of readers signed the petition.

Success In 1994, the local MP, Alan Milburn, introduced a bill into the House of Commons to scrap the year and a day rule, but it was narrowly defeated. However, following the delivery of the *Northern Echo*'s petition to the Law Commission (which makes proposals for reforming existing laws), a bill was passed by Parliament to become the 1996 Law Reform (Year and a Day Rule) Act.

The newspaper's role was vital in achieving success by mobilising public support. As its editor said, 'people were getting away with murder because the law was an ass. Newspapers have to do what they can to bring the law up to date.' However, because of the work of Michael's mother, we can also see this as a successful *individual* campaign.

Individual campaigns to affect policy making

Many campaigns that are later taken up by newspapers, politicians and pressure groups are started by a lone individual who feels strongly enough about a particular policy to take action themselves. The cases of Michael Brown's campaign for Clare's Law and Ann Ming's campaign to change the double jeopardy rule are good examples of where individuals began campaigns and persisted until they achieved change.

Clare's Law

In 2009, 36-year-old Clare Wood of Salford in Greater Manchester was beaten, raped and strangled, and her body set on fire by George Appleton, with whom she had previously been having a relationship. The relationship had ended in 2008 but Appleton had continued to harass her.

Unbeknown to Clare, Appleton had a history of convictions for violence against women, including a five-year prison sentence for holding an ex-girlfriend at knifepoint. He also had convictions for repeated harassment and threats, including four non-molestation orders relating to other women, and he had served six months in prison for breaching one of these orders. After killing Clare, Appleton went on the run and was later found hanged.

Protection Against Stalking

In 2011 Protection Against Stalking (PAS) launched a campaign to introduce a new law making stalking a specific offence. At that point, the existing 1997 anti-harassment law did not refer specifically to stalking. One estimate puts the number of victims at 120,000 a year.

In some cases, stalking leads to physical attacks and even deaths. Claire Bernal was shot dead by her stalker in 2005 while she was at work in a London department store. Her killer had been due in court the following week for harassing her.

Attitude of the justice system

The way the police were dealing with stalking was inadequate and haphazard. They lacked a clear policy and investigations were often left to individual officers' discretion. Victims were not being taken seriously and there were only 70 prosecutions in ten years under the 1997 Act.

The campaign

PAS concluded that the existing law was not fit for purpose. Supported by Napo, the probation officers' union, PAS set up an independent parliamentary inquiry, persuading MPs and peers (members of the House of Lords) from all parties to serve on it.

The inquiry lasted several months, hearing evidence from victims and their relatives (including mothers whose daughters had been killed by stalkers), academic experts, lawyers, police and probation officers. The inquiry heard about the intimidation, fear, and psychological and physical harm stalkers inflict and about the inadequate response of the authorities.

Success The inquiry's report was published in February 2012 with the support of 60 MPs and peers, the Police Federation and the Magistrates' Association. PAS were able to get support from MPs to include an amendment to a bill that was going through Parliament. This became the Protection of Freedoms Act in April 2012. It made stalking a criminal offence.

Reasons for success

The campaign succeeded in getting the law changed for several reasons. The inquiry allowed the voices of victims to be heard, as well as those from frontline practitioners in support organisations. They gained support from a wide range of important organisations and groups. They kept the campaign in the public eye through press releases to the media. They lobbied individual MPs and peers who could actually change the law. They gained support from all political parties.

ACTIVITY Media

Pressure group campaigning

Go to www.criminology.uk.net

INQUEST

The work of the pressure group INQUEST focuses on state-related deaths, such as those of people in police custody, prisons, immigration detention centres and psychiatric care. It has been involved in many inquests, including deaths in the Grenfell Tower fire, the 1989 Hillsborough disaster and the police shooting of Mark Duggan that preceded the 2011 London riots.

INQUEST campaigns to ensure that investigations into deaths treat bereaved people with dignity and respect. It is involved in a range of activities:

Casework INQUEST carries out specialist casework to support bereaved people so they can establish the truth about a death that has occurred while someone was in the care of the state.

Accountability INQUEST aims to ensure that state institutions are held accountable when they fail to safeguard those in their care.

Changing policies INQUEST aims to spread the lessons learnt from investigations in order to prevent further deaths. It gathers evidence from its casework, conducts research and uses its information to press public bodies to change their policies.

Examples of successful campaigns for policy changes by INQUEST include:

- Setting up the Independent Police Complaints Commission (IPCC), which investigates serious complaints and allegations of misconduct against the police.
- Extending the 2007 Corporate Manslaughter Act to cover deaths in the custody of public authorities (previously it only covered businesses).

INQUEST continues to campaign for changes, including:

- **Equal funding for bereaved families** at inquests into state-related deaths. Legal costs for public bodies at inquests are funded by the state but families have to pay their own costs.
- A '**Hillsborough Law**' to make it a crime for senior police officers to cover up institutional and individual failures.

NOW TEST YOURSELF

Practice Question

Discuss campaigns that have resulted in a change in law. (9 marks)

Source: WJEC Criminology Unit 2 examination 2018

Advice

You need to discuss two or more campaigns that have led to a change in the law, such as the campaigns covered in this Topic: campaigns for Sarah's Law and Clare's Law, the campaign against the double jeopardy law by Ann Ming, and Protection Against Stalking.

For each campaign that you deal with, briefly describe the situation that led to the campaign and how the campaign won support for a change in the law (through petitions, media support, backing from politicians etc.).

It is important that you state the name of the new law (e.g. the Domestic Violence Disclosure Scheme in the case of Clare's Law) and that you describe exactly what change in the law the campaign achieved.

Preparing for the Unit 2 exam

Now that you have completed Unit 2, you need to revise and prepare for the exam. This section will help you to get ready to tackle it. It contains some advice on preparing yourself, plus two past WJEC exam questions for you to try.

There is also advice on how to answer the questions, though you might want to try doing them without looking at the advice first.

Get organised!

The first thing to do is to get your file sorted out.

1. Make a list of all ten Unit 2 Topics to give you a framework for your revision.

2. Organise your notes, activities and homework for each Topic. Use the subheadings in each Topic as a guide to how to organise them. You could work with others and share your work or fill in any gaps you have together.

3. Make a list of the main issues covered in each Topic. Using these issues, go to your notes and textbook to find the material you need in order to understand them. Make any additional notes you need.

4. From your notes and textbook, list the key ideas that are needed for each Topic. Link these to the issues.

Practise, practise, practise!

Once you have your file in order, the best way to prepare for the exam is by practising the skill you're going to be tested on – the skill of answering exam questions. You wouldn't think of taking a driving test without doing any driving beforehand, and it's the same with exams.

Here are some ways you can practise:

Familiarise yourself with possible questions by looking at those in the *Now test yourself* sections at the end of each Topic and the practice paper on the next page.

Improve the answers you've already done. If you didn't get full marks on an assignment, re-write it, taking your teacher's comments on board, plus the advice in the *Now test yourself* section in the relevant Topic.

Answer any that you skipped earlier. You may not have done every assignment you were set. Do the ones you missed now. Your teacher might even mark them for you! If not, get a friend to give their opinion (and return the favour).

Study the student answers that appear at the end of some Topics and read the comments that go with them.

Answer past papers that you will find on the WJEC website (and while you're there, look at the mark schemes too).

End of Unit Practice Questions

Below are two questions from a past WJEC Criminology Unit 2 examination paper for you to answer. You will find advice on how to answer them on the next two pages. However, before looking at the advice, you might like to try making brief plans on how you would answer the questions. Alternatively, you can answer the questions first and then compare your answers with the advice afterwards.

QUESTION 1

Scenario

Martha has been married to Tony for 15 years. For most of that time she has been the victim of domestic abuse. For several reasons, she has never reported this to the police. The main reason is that she feels sorry for Tony as he has been unemployed for some time and cannot get a job. Tony gets upset about not being able to provide a better standard of living for Martha and himself. As a result of this, he has recently started to steal food from a local supermarket. Their neighbour knows about the domestic abuse and has recently seen a campaign on the television to promote awareness and encourage reporting of such abuse.

(a) (i)   Identify **one** sociological theory of criminality.   (1 mark)

(ii) Identify **three** features of the sociological theory of criminality named in question 1 (a) (i).   (3 marks)

(b) Explain how **one** sociological theory of criminality can be applied to Tony's situation.   (6 marks)

(c) Evaluate **one** sociological theory of criminality.   (9 marks)

(d) Other than sympathy, describe why victims of domestic abuse may not report the crime.   (6 marks)

Source: WJEC Criminology Unit 2 examination 2019

QUESTION 2

Scenario

Twin brothers Alan and Adrian are both campaigning for the position of Police and Crime Commissioner in their area. They are both concerned about the impact of the media's crime reporting on the public. They are both focusing their campaigns on crime control. Alan's crime control proposals focus on getting tough on crime and his campaign centres on penal populism. Adrian argues that individualistic theories of criminality should inform policy development. The twins' 80-year-old mother is very proud of her sons but cannot believe how much laws have changed in her lifetime.

(a) Identify **one** feature of formal policy making and **one** feature of informal policy making.   (2 marks)

(b) Briefly describe the crime control options that Alan might propose.   (4 marks)

(c) Briefly explain the impact of the media's representation of crime on the public perception
of crime.   (4 marks)

(d) Assess **one** crime control policy developed from individualistic theories of criminality.   (6 marks)

(e) Discuss how laws have changed over time.   (9 marks)

Source: WJEC Criminology Unit 2 examination 2019

Advice on answering the practice questions

Advice on answering Question 1

(a) (i) Just state the theory's name. Before choosing a theory to identify, look at question (a) (ii), where you will have to write about the sociological theory you have chosen.

(ii) Your answer depends on which theory you identified in (a) (i). For example, if you chose strain theory, you could identify these features:

- Society *socialises* its members into the goal of *'money success'*.
- But inequality means the working class *lack access to legitimate means* of achieving success (e.g. good schools).
- Their *blocked opportunities* create a *strain* between the goal and means of achieving it, leading to *anomie*.
- Individuals may respond in deviant ways, e.g. *'innovation'* – committing *utilitarian* crimes e.g. theft.

Use the key terms of your chosen theory (like the ones in italics above). Whichever theory you choose, link it to *criminality*.

(b) It may make sense to use the theory whose features you have already described. For example, if you chose strain theory, you could apply it as follows:

- Society sets the goal of material success for everyone, including Tony.
- But his opportunities to achieve this by legitimate means (e.g. hard work) are blocked because he is long-term unemployed.
- He feels the 'strain to anomie' because he cannot achieve the goal of a better standard of living.
- Tony responds by 'innovating', turning to utilitarian crime (theft of food) – an illegitimate means of achieving his goal.

Whichever theory you choose, stick to applying it to what is in the scenario. Don't make imaginary additions as to what else Tony might have done!

(c) This is an 'Evaluate' question focusing on the theory's strengths and limitations. Don't waste time describing the theory – you won't score any marks for this. Instead, focus on what it can or can't explain. You don't need an equal number of strengths and limitations, but you must say something about both. Use the relevant specialist vocabulary (like those in italics below). You can choose any sociological theory, but it may make sense to stick with the one you used for the previous question. For example, for strain theory, you could include:

Strengths/advantages

- It explains why *working-class crime rates* are higher: they are more likely to suffer *blocked opportunities* (e.g. lack of access to good schools, low-paid jobs) so they resort to *innovation* (*utilitarian crimes*, e.g. theft) to achieve success.
- It explains why individuals in different social positions resort to different *adaptations* (*conformity, innovation, ritualism, retreatism, rebellion*). E.g. the middle class are more likely to adopt conformity because they have more opportunity to succeed through *legitimate means*.

Limitations/disadvantages

- It ignores *crimes of the wealthy* and *ruling-class power* to make laws in their own interests.

- It is *deterministic*: not all working-class people commit crime.

- It sees crime solely as an *individual response*, ignoring *group criminality*, e.g. delinquent subcultures.

- It ignores *non-utilitarian crimes* with no economic motive, e.g. vandalism.

(d) This is a synoptic question and you must use your knowledge of Unit 1, Topic 1.2. There are several reasons for non-reporting, e.g. fear of further victimisation, lack of knowledge, shame/embarrassment or dependency. Cover several reasons. Develop your description of the reasons. For example, if the victim is dependent on the abuser, reporting the abuse risks losing their partner's financial support.

Advice on answering Question 2

(a) Identify formal policies as being official sanctions, such as fines or imprisonment to punish crime, or laws passed by Parliament. Informal policies can be thought of as unofficial sanctions, such as informal punishments in the family or peer group.

(b) Consider more than one crime control policy. Use the scenario to help you by building on the reference to the idea of 'getting tough on crime'. Explain what penal populism means and what policies it could involve, such as tougher prison sentences (e.g. longer or indeterminate sentences, or 'three strikes and you're out'). Other policies include tougher policing (e.g. zero tolerance) and situational crime prevention strategies (e.g. CCTV; target hardening). Link these policies to right realism (e.g. would-be offenders calculate the costs and benefits of offending, so making it more costly will deter them).

(c) This is a synoptic question, where you need to use your knowledge of Unit 1, Topic 1.5. Use key terms such as moral panic, stereotyping/typifications, folk devils, deviance amplification spiral, moral entrepreneurs to outline the media's representation of crime. Explain how media representation affects the public's view of crime. Does it create more fear of being a victim, or a false perception of crime trends as rising? Does it create negative attitudes to minorities or the young, or calls for tougher penalties for crimes that the media highlight? Mention any recent relevant examples and/or studies like Stanley Cohen's.

(d) Avoid lengthy descriptions of the theory itself and focus on the policy that comes from it. Policies include psychoanalysis (from Freud's theory), behaviour modification policies, e.g. token economies in prisons (from Skinner's operant learning theory), aversion therapy (from Eysenck's theory) and CBT programmes. This is an 'Assess' question so you must include positive and negative evaluations of the policy. For example, for token economies, briefly describe how it works, using specialist vocabulary (e.g. selective reinforcement). Consider how far it is effective, e.g. once reinforcement stops, behaviour begins to deteriorate, though more slowly than in prisoners who were not in the programme.

(e) Focus on changes in the laws over time, rather than on differences in laws between different societies or cultures – although you can discuss how cultural changes *within* a given society can lead to changes in the law. For example, you could discuss how changes in norms, values and attitudes *in British society* have led to changes in the laws on homosexuality – but avoid discussing how these laws or attitudes differ between Britain and *other societies'* views on homosexuality. Use examples of changes in particular laws, e.g. on drink driving, racism, homosexuality/LGBT+ rights, drugs or gun control. Describe the factors and steps that led to the change. Make sure you state the names of the laws (or penalties) that have changed.

References

Aichhorn, A (1925; 1936) *Wayward Youth*, Viking Press

Ariès, P (1960) *Centuries of Childhood*, Penguin

Baker, P et al (2013) 'Sketching Muslims: A corpus driven analysis of representations around the word 'Muslim' in the British press 1998–2009', *Applied Linguistics*

Ballinger S (ed) (2018) *1968-2018 Many Rivers Crossed*, British Future

Bandura, A et al (1963) 'Imitation of film-mediated aggressive models', *Journal of Abnormal and Social Psychology*

BBC News (2011)'Some England riot sentences "too severe"', BBC, 17 August

BBC News (2018) 'Police forces "ignoring Clare's Law and failing women"', BBC, 9 January

BBC News (2018) 'Stalking reports treble as prosecution rates fall', BBC, 20 July

Becker, H (1963) *Outsiders*, Free Press

Bennett, T and Wright, R (1984) *Remembering*, Cambridge University Press

Bowlby, J (1946; 1951) *Maternal Care and Maternal Health*, Shoken Books

Bradpiece, S (2016) 'Altered Perspectives: UK Rave Culture, Thatcherite Hegemony and the BBC', University of Bristol

Braithwaite, J (1988) *Crime, Shame and Reintegration*, Cambridge University Press

Carson, W (1971) 'White-Collar Crime and the Enforcement of Factory Legislation' in Carson W and Wiles P (eds) *Crime and Delinquency in Britain*, Martin Robertson

Casciani, D (2014) 'Crime stats: The truth is out there', BBC, 21 January

Chambliss, W (1975) 'Toward a Political Economy of Crime', *Theory and Society*

Christiansen, KO (1977) 'A Preliminary Study of Criminality among Twins', in Mednick, SA and Christiansen, KO (eds) *Biosocial Bases of Criminal Behaviour*, Gardiner Press

Cicourel, A (1968) *The Social Organisation of Juvenile Justice*, Wiley

Cloward, R and Ohlin, L (1960) *Delinquency and Opportunity*, The Free Press

Cohen, AK (1955) *Delinquent Boys*, The Free Press

Cohen, S (1972: 1973) *Folk Devils and Moral Panics*, Paladin

Downes, D and Hansen, K (2006) 'Welfare and punishment in comparative perspective' in Armstrong S et al (eds) *Perspectives on Punishment*, Oxford University Press

Durkheim, E (1893; 1964) *The Division of Labour in Society*, The Free Press

Elias, N (1978; 1982) *The Civilising Process*, Vols 1 and 2, Blackwell

Ellis, L and Coontz, P (1990) 'Androgens, Brain Functioning and Criminality', in Ellis, L and Hoffman, H (eds) *Crime in Biological, Social and Moral Contexts,* Praeger

Eysenck, HJ (1952) 'The Effects of Psychotherapy: An Evaluation', *Journal of Consulting Psychology*

Eysenck, HJ (1964) *Crime and Personality*, RKP

Farrington, DP et al (1982) 'Personality and Delinquency in London and Montreal', in Gunn, J and Farrington, DP (eds) *Abnormal Offenders, Delinquency and the Criminal Justice System*, Wiley

Feeley, M and Simon, J (1994) 'Actuarial Justice' in Nelken, D *The Futures of Criminology*, Sage

Feldman, MP (1977) *Criminal Behaviour: a psychological analysis*, Wiley

Felson, M (2012) *Crime and Everyday Life*, Pine Forge Press

Gesch, CB et al (2002) 'Influence of Supplementary Vitamins, Minerals and Essential Fatty Acids on the Antisocial Behaviour of Young Adult Prisoners', *British Journal of Psychiatry*

Glueck, S and Glueck, E (1950) *Unravelling Juvenile Delinquency*, Commonwealth Fund

Goffman, E (1961) *Asylums*, Doubleday

Gottfredson, M and Hirschi, T (1990) *A General Theory of Crime*, Stanford University Press

Green, P and Ward, T (2005) 'Special Issue on State Crime', *British Journal of Criminology*

Haggerty, K and Ericson, R (2000) 'The Surveillant Assemblage', *British Journal of Sociology*

Henry, S and Milovanovic, D (1996) *Constitutive Criminology*, Sage

Hirschi and Gottfredson (1990) 'Commentary: Testing the General Theory of Crime', *Journal of Research in Crime and Delinquency*

Home Office (2003) *The Crime and Justice Survey*

Hutchings, B and Mednick, SA (1977) 'Registered criminality in the adoptive and biological parents of registered male criminal adoptees', in Fieve, RR et al (eds) *Genetic Research in Psychiatry*, Johns Hopkins University Press

Ishikawa, S, Raine, A et al (2001) 'Autonomic stress reactivity and executive functions in successful and unsuccessful criminal psychopaths from the community', *Journal of Abnormal Psychology*

Jacob, PA et al (1965) 'Aggressive Behaviour, Mental Sub-normality and the XYY Male', *Nature*

Jeffery, C (1959) 'An Integrated Theory of Crime and Criminal Behaviour', *Journal of Criminal Law, Criminology and Police Science*

Kaspersson, M (2008) 'On Treating the Symptoms and not the Cause: Reflections on the Dangerous Dogs Act', *Papers from the British Criminology Conference 2008*

Kelley, N and Sharrock, S (2017) *Racial prejudice in Britain today*, NatCen

Kohlberg, L (1976) 'Moral stages and moralisation: The cognitive-developmental approach', in Lickona T (ed) *Moral Development and Behavior*, Holt, Reinhart & Winston

Lea, J and Young, J (1984; 1993) *What is to be Done About Law and Order?* Penguin

Lemert, E (1972) *Human Deviance, Social Problems and Social Control*, Prentice-Hall

Lodge, M and Hood, C (2002) 'Pavlovian policy responses to media feeding frenzies? Dangerous dogs regulation in comparative perspective', *Journal of Contingencies and Crisis Management*

Lombroso, C (1897) *L'Uomo Delinquente*, Bocca

Males, M and Macallair, D (1998) 'The effect of juvenile curfew laws in California', *Western Criminological Review*

Matthews, VM (1968) 'Differential Association: an empirical note', *Social Problems*

Mednick, SA et al (1984) 'Genetic Influences on Criminal Convictions', *Science*

Merton, RK (1938; 1949) 'Social Structure and Anomie' in Anshen R (ed) *The Family*, Harper Brothers

Murray, C (1990) *The Emerging British Underclass*, IEA

Norris, C (2012) 'Accounting for the global growth of CCTV' in Ball, K et al (eds) *Routledge Handbook of Surveillance Studies*, Routledge

Norris, C and Armstrong, G (1999) *The Maximum Surveillance Society*, Berg

Osborn, SG and West, DJ (1979) 'Conviction records of fathers and sons compared', *British Journal of Criminology*

Pew Global Attitudes Survey (2013) 'The Global Divide on Homosexuality', Pew Research Center

Piliavin, I and Briar, B (1964) 'Police Encounters with Juveniles', *American Journal of Sociology*

Price, WH and Whatmore, PB (1967) 'Behaviour Disorders and Patterns of Crime among XYY Males', *British Medical Journal*

Rettig, S (1966) 'Ethical risk taking in group and individual conditions', *Journal of Personality and Social Psychology*

Rogers, S (2012), 'Riots broken down: who was in court and what's happened to them?' The Guardian, 4 July

Sammons, A and Putwain, D (2018) *Psychology and Crime*, Routledge

Scarmella, T and Brown, W (1978) 'Serum testosterone and aggressiveness in hockey players', *Psychosomatic Medicine*

Schalling (1987) 'Personality correlates of testosterone levels in young delinquents', in Mednick SA et al (eds) *The Causes of Crime: New Biological Approaches*, Cambridge University Press

Schlesinger, P and Tumber, H (1992) 'Crime and Criminal Justice in the Media', in Downes, D *Unravelling Criminal Justice*, Macmillan

Schoenthaler, SJ (1982) 'The effects of blood sugar on the treatment and control of anti-social behaviour', *International Journal of Biosocial Research*

Sheldon, WH (1940) *Varieties of Delinquent Youth*, Harper

Siddique, H (2016) 'England had 5,700 recorded cases of FGM in 2015-16, figures show', The Guardian, 21 July

Skinner, BF (1953) *Science and Human Behavior*, Macmillan

Sutherland, E (1949) *White Collar Crime*, Holt, Rinehart and Winston

Thornton, D and Reid, RL (1982) 'Moral reasoning and types of criminal offence', *British Journal of Social Psychology*

Tombs, S (2013) 'Corporate crime', in Hale C et al (eds) *Criminology*, Oxford University Press

Wilkins, L (1964) *Social Deviance*, Tavistock

Wilson, J and Herrnstein, R (1985) *Crime and Human Nature*, Simon and Schuster

Wilson, J and Kelling, G (1982) 'Broken Windows', *Atlantic Monthly*

Yochelson, S and Samenow, S (1976) *The Criminal Personality*, Jason Aronson

Young, J (1971) *The Drugtakers*, Paladin

Young, J (2002) 'Crime and social exclusion' in Maguire, M et al (eds) *The Oxford Handbook of Criminology*, Oxford University Press